Ralph Bigland

Observations on marriages, baptisms, and burials,

As preserved in parochial registers. With sundry specimens of the entries

of marriages, baptisms, &c. in foreign countries: interspersed with divers

remarks concerning proper methods necessary to pres

Ralph Bigland

Observations on marriages, baptisms, and burials,
As preserved in parochial registers. With sundry specimens of the entries of marriages, baptisms, &c. in foreign countries: interspersed with divers remarks concerning proper methods necessary to pres

ISBN/EAN: 9783337775261

Printed in Europe, USA, Canada, Australia, Japan

Cover: Foto ©ninafisch / pixelio.de

More available books at **www.hansebooks.com**

OBSERVATIONS

ON

MARRIAGES,

BAPTISMS, and BURIALS,

AS PRESERVED IN

PAROCHIAL REGISTERS.

WITH

Sundry Specimens of the Entries of MARRIAGES, BAPTISMS, &c. in foreign Countries: Interfperfed with divers Remarks concerning proper Methods neceffary to preferve a Remembrance of the feveral Branches of Families, &c.

By RALPH BIGLAND, Efq; Somerfet Herald.

LONDON:

Printed by W. RICHARDSON and S. CLARK, in Fleet-ftreet;
And fold by R. and J. DODSLEY, in Pall-mall; T. PAYNE, at the Mews Gate, Charing-Crofs; J. STEPHENS, between the Temple Gates; W. BRISTOW, in St. Paul's Church-yard; and H. PAYNE, at Dryden's Head in Pater-nofter-Row.

MDCCLXIV.

[Price Three Shillings.]

HERALDS OFFICE, May 1, 1764.

Shortly will be Published in Numbers,

BARONAGIUM ANGLIÆ;

SIVE

STEMMATA NOBILITATIS ANGLICANÆ:

Exhibiting, in a regular Series of Descents,

The GENEALOGIES of the ENGLISH NOBILITY,

With Historical Notes occasionally introduced.

EMBELLISHED WITH

Escutcheons of Arms, Crests, Supporters, Mottos, Badges, &c.

The Whole confirmed by authentic Monuments of Antiquity preserved in the Public Offices of the Kingdom, particularly in the College of Arms.

By { RALPH BIGLAND, Esq; Somerset
AND
ISAAC HEARD, Esq; Lancaster } Heralds.

This Work will be rendered still more complete by the Addition of the DESCENTS of the several HEIRESSES,

(A Plan hitherto unattempted)

WHEREBY

The extensive Alliances of each NOBLE FAMILY, additional Titles, Hereditary Honours, Assumption of Arms, Claims to, and Inheritance of Estates, &c. &c. will be further illustrated.

CONDITIONS.

I. THIS WORK will be printed in Folio upon a large superfine Imperial Paper, and will make about FIFTY Numbers.

II. EACH NUMBER, containing EIGHT Pages, stitched in Blue, will be published as often as the Nature of the Work will admit, Price FOUR SHILLINGS.

III. EACH SUBSCRIBER to pay TWO GUINEAS in Advance on account of the great Expence that will attend the Execution of the Work; this Money will be allowed in the Numbers delivered.

IV. A LIST of the Subscribers will be Printed.

The NOBILITY and GENTRY who are inclined to patronize this Work, are desired to send their Names and Subscription-Money as early as possible to the COMPILERS at the Heralds Office, by whom the Numbers will be regularly delivered, as well as by the following Booksellers;

R. and J. DODSLEY, in Pall-mall.
R. DAVIS, in Piccadilly.
J. ROBSON, in New Bond-street.
J. GRETTON, in Old Bond-street.
T. PAYNE, at the Mews Gate.
T. DAVIES, in Russell-street, Covent-Garden.
W. BATHOE, in the Strand.
A. WEBLEY, in Holborn.

J. STEPHENS, between the Temple Gates.
T. SNELLING, in Fleet-street.
G. KEARSLEY, in Ludgate-street.
J. RIVINGTON, } St. Paul's Church-yard.
W. BRISTOW, }
H. PAYNE, in Pater-noster-Row.
T. FIELD, the upper End of Cheapside.
RICHARDSON and URQUHART, at the Royal Exchange.

Where SPECIMENS of the Work may be seen.

OF

PAROCHIAL REGISTERS, &c.

RESPECTING CHIEFLY

Their UTILITY and CONSERVATION,

For the Benefit of POSTERITY.

HE necessity of proper RECORDS, authenticated by public Parochial Registers, more particularly for ascertaining the MARRIAGES, BIRTHS, BAPTISMS, DEATHS, and BURIALS, of persons within their respective Parishes, is abundantly evident from a transient view of our ancient English History, which, for want of proper NAMES, and real DATES, and FAMILY CONNECTIONS, occasionally to be referred to, is oftentimes rendered perplexed and unintelligible, and sometimes altogether inconsistent even with its own Chronology.

This defect, so often heretofore complained of, was at last happily removed by that great politician Thomas Cromwell (afterwards Earl of Essex) when, being the king's vicar-general, he in the year 1538 ordered it to the clergy throughout England, that in their respective parishes a public REGISTER should be kept for the above purposes: and this order of Cromwell was continued in the several injunctions of King Edward VI. Queen Elizabeth, and King James I. particularly in that of Queen Elizabeth, every minister at institution was, among other things, to subscribe to this protestation; *I shall keep the Register Booke according to the queene's majesties injunction.*

It was chiefly from the want of such method of registering the Family SURNAMES, that the sons of one and the same common father were heretofore so diversely distinguished, as I shall hereafter shew.

" NAMES, called in Latin NOMINA, quasi NOTAMINA (says the learned Camden) " were first imposed for the dis-
" tinction of persons, which we now call Christian Names;
" after, for difference of families, which we call SURNAMES,
" and have been especially respected, as whereon the glory
" and credit of men is grounded, and by which the same is
" conveyed to the knowledge of posterity, and that every
" person had in the beginning one only proper name, as
" Adam, Joseph, &c. &c."

Camden

Camden obferves, he never could find an hereditary furname in England before the conqueft: the furnames in Doomfday Book were brought in by the Normans, who not long before had taken them; but they were moftly noted with a DE, as John de Babington, Walter de Hugget, Nicholas de Yateman, &c. or Ricardus filius Roberti, &c. and that they were not fettled among the common people till about the reign of King Edward II. SURNAMES, not from SIRE, but becaufe fuper-added to the Chriftian Name. Places anciently gave names to perfons, and not the contrary: William fon of Roger Fitz Valerine, in the time of King Henry I. being born in the caftle of Howard in Wales, did from thence affume the name of the place of his birth, and tranfmitted the fame to his pofterity. Edward of Caernarvon, fo called from the place of his nativity; fo Thomas of Brotherton, from the Village in Yorkfhire wherein he was born; and John of Gaunt, from the city of Gaunt in Flanders, where he was born.

Herne fuppofes that Surnames were as old as King Jna, about 680, and inftances in Ethelheard Umming, an Anglo-Saxon, and that the name defcended to his pofterity, like as Cumming or Cumin to this day, and blames Camden for fuppofing the contrary.

William ap Thomas, ap Gillim, ap Jenkin, when made Earl of Pembroke by King Edward IV. took the name of Herbert, becaufe an anceftor of his in King Henry Ift's time was fo called;

called; another from the name of the principal family manor, as Cavendish, son of Gernon. Nigell de Albini, by gift of King Henry I. possessing the lands of Robert de Mowbray, Earl of Northumberland (who was attainted) his posterity by the king's command took the surname and arms of Mowbray. The custom of taking names from towns and villages in England is a sufficient proof of the ancient descents of those families who are still inhabitants of the same places, as Lowther of Lowther, Standish of Standish, Errington of Errington, Stonor of Stonor, Kingscote of Kingscote, Towneley of Towneley, and many others too numerous to mention. John Horsley marrying the heiress of the ancient Delavals, his son James took the name and arms of his mother, and from whom the present Delavals of Seaton Delaval. Another from the office he sustained, as Usher the son of Nevil; Marshal, from being marshal of the king's palace; whence the Marshals Earls of Pembroke. De Mora, of the Moor; whence St. Maur, now Seymour; and Otho, alias Windsor, from being castellan of Windsor-castle: others took their names from forests, as Percy, so called from Percy-forest, in the province of Maine, and not (as Camden observes) from piercing the king of Scots through the eye; others from woods, as the family of Bosco or Bois, formerly of Fersfield in Norfolk, from the great wood that adjoined to their mansion; others from hills, dales, &c. from trees, as Coigners (Conyers) from the quince-tree; others from the oak, beech, elm, pine, vine, &c. others from rivers, as Tyne, Eden, Derwent, &c. others from fishes, as salmon,

herring,

herring, whiting, haddock, trout, &c. and in respect of stature, learning, colour, and other causes. Camden gives us a remarkable instance of one family, which he took from an old roll that did belong to Sir William Brereton of Brereton, in Cheshire, Knt. as follows:

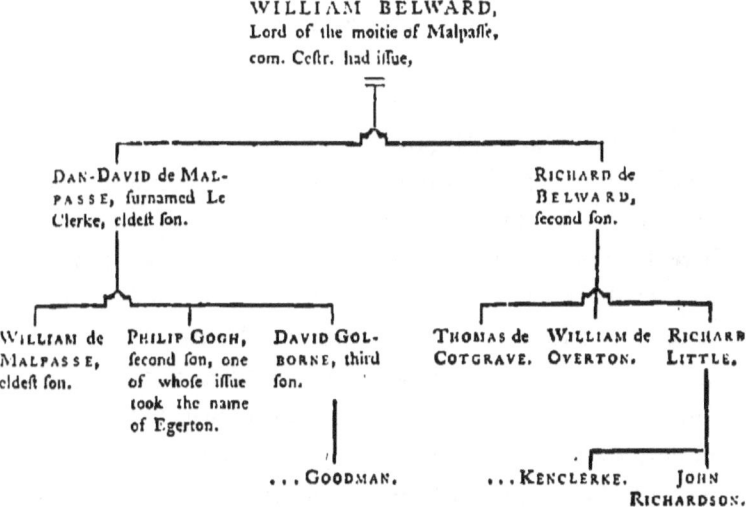

By this remarkable example of the alteration of names in early times it is, that at this day many families, who have neglected to keep up their pedigrees, are at a loss to account for the similar bearing of arms, whose names are so widely different, while yet they might all originally be descended from one and the same common ancestor. Little (for instance) would any one think to look for the family and arms of Botteville

teville in the prefent ~~Earl of~~ ^Viscount Weymouth; and this only, becaufe in the time of King Edward IV. John de Botteville re-
fided at one of the inns of court, and from thence was named
John of Th' Inne (Thynne); and as little would he fufpect
that that poor ^deferted and expofed infant at Newark upon Trent, commonly called
Tom among us, fhould afterwards be metamorphofed into the
great Dr. Thomas Magnus, that famous non-refident and am-
baffador.

From the want of Regifters of Chriftian names it has happened that one perfon has been often put for another: Godwin, in his De Præfulibus Angliæ, makes William Sever to
have been warden of Merton, bifhop of ~~Chichefter~~ ^Carlifle, and afterwards bifhop of Durham, when the warden and the bifhop
were two diftinct perfons; Henry and William, who lived
and died in diftinct centuries: fuch miftakes from the near
fimilitude of names reminds me of the comment I once heard
made by a perfon upon the reading of St. Paul's * preaching
before Fælix, " Ay, fee how very different he here is from
" what he once was, when he perfecuted the prophet David!"
hereby making in the Sacred Hiftory an anachronifm of only
about eleven hundred years.

That fuch arbitrary alterations and cafual impofition of
names is contrary to true policy, as what, by introducing con-

* Alfo called Saul.

fufion

fufion in families, may alfo eventually introduce confufion in the ftate, might be fhewn, if neceffary, in various inftances; of which the parliament of Paris were fo fenfible, that they paffed an act purpofely againft it, unlefs in cafes where eftates were left charged with fuch conditions.

Although the utility of REGISTERS, for afcertaining the true æra of time and perpetuating the exact hiftory of family connexions, is fo abundantly evident, yet might they be rendered ftill MORE USEFUL, if the feveral entries therein made were more particular; for inftance, in the entry of a Marriage, if the Chriftian names, &c. of the fathers and mothers of the married couple, together with their degrees, occupations, and their refpective places of real habitation, were particularly fpecified (as I fhall prefume by examples hereafter) it would at once clearly determine the defcent of the iffue by fuch marriage, and enable pofterity to trace their pedigrees with great exactnefs, and by the moft authentic proof.

It is much to be lamented, that during Cromwell's ufurpation few Parochial Regifters were kept with any tolerable regularity; yet I have now a Regifter before me of that time, which gives the feveral particulars as above required, in the following entry:

" MEMORANDUM: That the intended marriage between
" Richard Mallett of Sutton Mallett, in the countie of Som-
" merfett,

"merfett, gentleman (now an officer in the ftanding army) the fonne of Francis Mallett, fome tyme of Sutton Mallett, in the countie of Sommerfett aforefaid, gentleman, deceafed, and of Elizabeth his relict, now living in the parifh and countie aforefaid, of the one part; and Sufanna Newbery, fpinfter, daughter of Henry Newbery, efquier, and of Frances his wife, both now living in the town of .... and countie of .... of the other part, was publifhed on three feveral Lords days in the parifh church; that is to fay, on the 3d, 10th, 17th Decemb. no exception was made againft the fame."

At this time particularly a perfon was elected by the parifhioners to the office of Regifter, as appears by the certificate of Robert Tichborne, alderman of London, taken from the Regifter that did formerly belong to the parifh church of St. Peter, now united to St. Benet, Paul's Wharf, London, as follows:

"Thefe are to certify whom it may concern, that on the 23d day of September 1653, before me Robert Tichborne, alderman, one of the juftices of the peace within the city, came Thomas French of the Parifh of Peeter's Poul's Wharfe, and produced a certificate under the hand of feveral of the inhabitants of the parifh aforefaid of his election upon the 20th day of this inftant September, by them to the place of Regifter for Marriages, Births, and Burials, in the parifh "afore-

" aforesaid, according to an act of parliament in that case
" made and provided, desiring my approbation of the said
" Thomas French to the place of regiſtering aforesaid, as also
" to swear him to the said Office, as is by the said act di-
" rected; both which I have accordingly done. Witneſs my
" hand the day and year abovesaid.

ROBERT TICHBORNE."

And under this entry,

"MARRIADGES
" Begone the 30 of September 1653.

" John Ridgway, bricklar, and Mary Chart, widdow, ac-
" cording to a act of parliament baringe date the 24 Auguſt
" 1653 was three several times publiſſed in the market-place
" and afterwarde maried by mee upon Tuesday the six of
" December 1653.

THOMAS ATKIN."

Arundel, in Suſſex, 1653.

" Thomas Ballard, Gent. Town-Regiſter, sworn before
" me John Albery, Mayor.

"MARRIAGES.

1653,   " John Turner of Steyning, Suſſex, and Sarah
March 9. " Campion of Sounting, in the said county, spinſter,
           " with consent of friends. Publiſhed in Steyning
           " and Sounting."

D

1654,

1654, " John Blundell of Charlewood, in Surrey, mercer,
Apr. vi. " and Eleanor Mills of Pulburrough, in Suffex, fpin-
" fter, above 21 years of age, with confent of friends.
" Publifhed in Charlewood and Pulburrough."

From another Regifter.

" MEMORANDUM: That the marriage between John Hob-
" fon of ..... in this county, gentleman, late the fon of Ro-
" bert Hobfon, late of Oram, alias Utram, in the county of
" Yorke, deceafed, of the one part, and Lucy St. Paul of
" Hammerfmith in the parifh of Fulham, in the county of
" Middlefex, widowe, of the other part, was folemnized be-
" fore Colonel Harvey, one of the juftices of the peace of this
" common wealth, on the 28 day of June, according to a
" late act of parliament concerning marriages, 1654."

Certificate of a marriage performed before Sir John Dethick, Knt. Alderman of London.

" LONDON, ff. According to an act of parliament, intituled,
" An Act for Marriages, and the Regiftering thereof, and
" alfo touching Births and Burials, I John Dethick, Knight,
" one of the aldermen and juftices of the peace for the faid
" cittye, doe hereby certifie unto all whom it may concerne,
" That Robert Conftable of Andrewes Holborne, Gent. and
" Bridget Exton of the parifh of Benet's Paul's Wharfe, pro-
" ducing two certificates under the hands of the refpective
" Regifters

"Reglfters of the publication of their intention of marrying
"each with other three feveral market-dayes, in Newgate-
"market, in three feveral weekes, were married before me
"the tenth day of November 1656, in the prefence of John
"Exton, doctor of the civil lawe, father of the faid Bridget,
"Everard Exton, Mary Exton, and John Clements of Lon-
"don, Gent. and other witneffes. In teftimony whereof I have
"hereunto fett my hand and feale the 11 day of November
"1656.
                                                J^{no} DETHICK."

The Reverend and ingenious Richard Burn, L. L. D. vicar of Orton in Weftmorland, in his Ecclefiaftical Law, obferves, "that an act of parliament was thought neceffary, after "the Grand Rebellion, to intitle people who had been mar- "ried by juftices of the peace to fuch legal advantages of "dower, thirds, and the like, as attended marriages duly fo- "lemnized according to the rites of the church of England."

But the moft remarkable entries I have feen, I fhall beg leave, for their fingularity, to introduce from a copy formerly taken from the Parifh Regifter of St. Botolph Aldgate; as follow :

"Michell Didyer, a ftranger, born at Marfeilles in Pro- "vence, a pilot under Mr. Candifh in his voyage to the South "Endyes, and Jaquete Defheaz, a maiden, born in Jerfey, "married 2d November 1588."

" Thomas Speller, a dumb perſon, by trade a ſmith, of
" Hatfield Broadoake, in the county of Eſſex, and Sarah Earle,
" daughter to one John Earle of Great Paringdon, in the
" ſame county, yeoman, were married by licence granted by
" Doctor Edwards, chancellor of the dioces of London, the
" ſeaventh day of November, anno Dni 1618, which licence
" aforeſaid was granted at the requeſt of Sir Francis Barring-
" ton, Knight, and others of the place above-named, who by
" their letters certified Mr. Chancellor that the parents of ei-
" ther of them had given their conſents to the ſaid marriage,
" and the ſaid Thomas Speller the dumb parties willingneſs
" to have the ſame performed, appeared by taking the book
" of Common Prayer and his lycence in one hand and his
" bride in the other, and coming to Mr. John Briggs, our
" miniſter and preacher, and made the beſt ſigns he could to
" ſhew that he was willing to be married, which was then
" performed accordinglie; and alſo the ſaid lord chief juſtice
" of the King's Bench, as Mr. Briggs was informed, was made
" acquainted with the ſaid marriage before it was ſolemnized,
" and allowed it to be lawful.—This marriage is ſet down at
" large, becauſe we never had the like before."

" July 17, 1655. William Clark, ſon to John Clark, a ſol-
" dier, and Thomaſine his wife, who herſelf went for a ſoul-
" dier, and was billetted at the Three Hammers in Eaſt Smith-
" field, about ſeven months, and after was delivered of this
" child the 16th day of this July, and was baptized the 17th
" in

"in her lodging, being one Mr. Hubber's houfe: fhe had been a fouldier by her own confeffion about five years, and was fome time drummer to the company."

Such particulars as thefe to identify the perfons regiftered, are certainly proper; but the moft remarkable for exactnefs I have feen for a baptifm is the following:

"Upon Monday, 26 October 1663, the only fon of Sir John Clopton of Clopton, in the county of Warwick, Knt. by his wife Barbara, daughter and heire of Sir Edward Walker, Knt. Garter principal king of arms, was baptized Edward, by Dr. John Earles, Bifhop of Salifbury, in Garter's lodgings in the heralds office, fituate in the parifh of St. Benet Paul's Wharf, London."

To thefe I fhall add a remarkable paffage from the parifh regifter-book of Frocefter, in the county of Glocefter, being a literal copy; viz.

"Hoc anno 1574, die Laurentii Martyris, fereniffima regina mea Elizabetha hoc meum oppidatum acceffit & invifit in eoq; in ædibus Georgii Huntleii armigeri comiter, benigneq; & fuma cum humanitate tractantis pernoctavit indeq; Barkleyum caftellum conceffit.

     Tho. Tullio, vicario de Frocefter.
Gulielmo Pegler, }
Johan. Wilkins, } Gardianis."

By this circumſtance we find that the moſt private villages ſometimes obtain a remembrance from the birth or reſidence of ſome great perſonage, and that on the feaſt of St. Laurence the Martyr, in the year 1574, her majeſty Queen ELIZABETH honoured the village of Froceſter with her royal preſence, and reſted at the manſion-houſe of George Huntley, Eſq; in her way to Berkeley-caſtle. Though this may not properly belong to entries in Pariſh Regiſters, yet ſuch anecdotes or memorials occaſionally introduced upon remarkable events, are not amiſs, as they frequently tend to elucidate matters of greater moment.

The Funeral Certificates of the NOBILITY and GENTRY of this kingdom, as regiſtered in the HERALDS OFFICE, together with their arms, quarterings, and ſupporters, elegantly depicted and duly regulated, are ſome of the fineſt records extant, and will be ſtanding monuments of the caution and concern families had to tranſmit their connexions, feats in war, and honourable enſigns to poſterity; but this good cuſtom, formerly ſo well eſtabliſhed to preſerve their memories from oblivion, and anſwer the good ends intended, is now much neglected: however, as examples for imitation and the informtaion of thoſe who are unacquainted with this manner of regiſtering of families, I ſhall here preſent the following, extracted from the originals:

FUNERAL

FUNERAL CERTIFICATES.

THOMAS CLINTON, Earl of LINCOLN.

The Right Honourable THOMAS Earle of Lincolne departed this mortall life the 15th daye of January 1618, at his houfe at Tatterfhal, in the countye of Lincolne, and was buried in the chauncell of the church of Tatterfhall aforefaide. He maried ELIZABETH, daughter and coheire of Sir Henry Knevitt of Charlton, in the countye of Wilts, Knt. by whom he had yffue, Katherine, eldeft daughter, who dyed without yffue; Elizabeth, 2d daughter; Frances, 3d daughter; Henry, eldeft fonne, Thomas, 2d fonne, both dyed without yffue; Arabella, 4th daughter; Theophilus, fonne and heire, now Earle of Lincolne; Edward, 4th fonne; Lucy and Anne, both dyed without yffue; Charles, 5th fonne; Knevitt, 6th fonne; Sufan, 7th daughter; Robert, 7th fonne, dyed without yffue; John, 8th fonne; Dorcas, 8th daughter; and Sarah, 9th and youngeft daughter. This certificate was taken the laft daye of April 1619, by Sampfon Lennard, Blewe Mantle.

ELIZABETH HASTINGS, Countefs of WORCESTER.

The Right Honourable Lady ELIZABETH HASTINGS, late Counteffe of Worcefter, and daughter of the Right Honourable Francis Earle of Huntingdon, departed this mortall life at Worcefter-houfe in the Strand, London, the 24th daye of Auguft 1621, whofe corpes was conveyed ymmediately following from thence to Ragland, in the countye of Monmouth, there to be interred. She was maried to the Right Honourable EDWARD Earle of Worcefter, Lord Privie Seale, by whom fhe had yffue, William Lord Herbert, eldeft fonne, that dyed without yffue; Henry, nowe Lord Herbert, 2d fonne and heire; Sir Thomas Somerfett, 3d fonne, Knight of the Bath; Sir Charles Somerfett, 4th fonne, Knight of the Bath; Sir Edward Somerfett, 5th fonne, Knight of the Bath; and Chriftopher, youngeft fonne; and five daughters; Elizabeth, eldeft daughter, maried to Sir Henry Guildford of the countye of Kent, Knt. Katharine, 2d daughter, maried to William Lord Petre; Anne, 3d daughter, maried to Sir Edward Winter of Lidney, in the countye of Glocester, Knt. Frances, 4th daughter, to William Morgan of Lanternam, in the countye of Monmouth, Esq; Blanch, 5th daughter, maried to Thomas, sonne and heire of the Lord Arundel of Wardour; and Katharine, youngest daughter, maried to Thomas Lord Windsor; Henry Lord Herbert, and baron of parliament, maried Anne, daughter and sole heire of John Lord Russell, sonne and heire of Francis Earle of Bedford, by whom he had yssue six sonnes and three daughters; Edward, the eldest sonne and heire; John, 2d sonne; Henry, 3d sonne; Thomas, 4th; Charles, 5th, and James, the 6th sonne; Anne, eldest daughter; Mary, and Elizabeth; Sir Thomas Somerset, 3d sonne, maried the Countesse of Ormond, and hath yssue, Elizabeth, a daughter; Sir Charles Somerset, 4th sonne, maried the daughter and heire of Sir William Powell of the countye of Monmouth, Knt. and hath yet no yssue; Sir Edward Somerset and Christopher, youngest sonnes, both dyed without yssue.

RICHARD SACKEVILLE, Earl of DORSET.

The Right Honourable RICHARD SACKEVILLE, Earle of Dorset, sonne of Robert Earle of Dorset, the sonne of Thomas first Earle of Dorset and Lord High Treasurer of England, departed this mortall life at Dorset-house by Fleet-street, in London, on Easter-day the xxviii[th] of March 1624; whose body was honourably conveyed through the city of London on Tuesday night the 6th daye of April following unto Buckhurst in Sussex, and there buried in the parish church of Withiam with his ancestors, in a vault belonging only to that family. He maried Lady ANNE, only-daughter and heire of George Clifford, Earle of Cumberland; by whom he had yssue one sonne and two daughters; Thomas Sackeville Lord Buckherst, his sonne and heire, who dyed in his infancy; Lady Margaret, eldest daughter, borne 2 daye of July 1614, and Lady Isabella, borne 6 of October 1622, both living at the time of their father's death. The heire male unto all his honours is Sir Edward Sackeville, Knight, his 2 brother,

nowe

nowe Earle of Dorſet and Lord Buckhurſt. This certificate was taken by Sampſon Lennard, Blew Mantle.

KATHARINE SOMERSET, Lady PETRE.

The Right Honourable Lady KATHARINE SOMERSET, 2d daughter of Edward Earle of Worceſter, Lord Privy Seal, and wife unto the Right Honourable Lord WILLIAM PETRE, Baron Petre, of Writtle in Eſſex, departed this mortall life at Thornden (my Lord's houſe in Eſſex aforeſaid) upon the laſt daye of October, anno Dom. 1624, and was buried in the church of Ingerſtone, within a chapel erected for my Lord's family, and under a monument formerly prepared for my Lord and her. My Lord hath yſſue by her, livinge at the tyme of her death, ſeven ſonnes; viz. Robert Petre, now eldeſt and heire apparent, who hath wedded Mary, daughter of the Right Honourable Anthony Viſcount Montacute, of Cowdrey in Suſſex; William, 2d ſonne; Edward, 3d; John, 4th; Thomas, 5th; Henry, 6th; George, 7th ſonne; and three daughters; viz. Elizabeth, wife of William Sheldon, of Beoley in com. Worceſter, Eſquire; Mary, married to the Right Honorable John Lord Teynham, of Teynham in Kent; Katharine, married to John Carrell, ſonne and heire apparent of Sir John Carrell, of Harting in Suſſex, Knt. John Petre, firſt-born ſonne, and a daughter, named Anne, dyed both young. This certificate was taken by John Philipot, alias Somerſet, the firſt day of December 1624.

MARY NEVILLE, Baroneſs LE DESPENCER.

The Right Honourable Lady MARY Baroneſs LE DESPENCER, ſole daughter and heire to the Right Honourable Sir Henry Neville, Knt. Baron of Abergaveny, and widow of Sir THOMAS FANE, of Badſell in Kent, Knt. departed this mortall life at her caſtle of Meerworth, in the county of Kent aforeſaid, upon the xxviii[th] day of June 1626, and her funeral obſequies with great honour, and with all things requiſite to her degree, were performed by her heire, being her ſole executor, at the ſaid caſtle and church of Meerworth, vpon the 14 day of

F   July

July next following, her corps being interred in the chauncel there. She had yffue by the faid Sir Thomas Fane as followeth; her eldeft fon and heire Francis Fane, made Knt. of the Bath at the coronation of King James, and after, in the 22d year of his majefty's raigne, in the life-tyme of his faid mother, he was created Baron Bergherft and Earl of Weftmorland, who by Mary his wife, fole daughter and heire of Sir Antony Mildmay of Apthorp, in the county of Northampton, Knt. and of Grace his wife, daughter and coheire of Sir Henry Sherington of Lacock, in com. Wilts, Knt. hath yffue as followeth; viz. fix fonnes and fix daughters; firft, Mildmay Fane, made Knight of the Bath at the coronation of King Charles, then called Lord Burgherfh, but fince the deceafe of his faid grandmother ftiled Lord Le Defpencer, newly married to Grace Thornihurft, daughter of Sir William Thornihurft, of Herne in Kent, Knt. and of Anne his wife, one of the two fifters and coheires of Lord Thomas Howard, Vifcount Bindon; Lady Grace, eldeft daughter, married to the Right Honourable James Earle Humes of Scotland; Lady Mary, 2d; Lady Elizabeth, 3d; Lady Rachel, 4th; Lady Frances, 5th; and Lady Katharine, 6th; Sir Francis, 2d fonne to the Earle of Weftmorland, made Knight of the Bath at the coronation of King Charles; Antony, 3d fonne; George, 4th fonne; William, 5th fonne; Robert, 6th fonne; Sir George Fane of Burfton in Kent, Knt. 2d fonne to the faid defunct lady, married to his firft wife Elizabeth, daughter to the Right Honourable Robert Lord Spencer of Wormleyton, who dying without any yffue furviving her, he re-married to his 2d wife Anne, daughter of Sir Oliver Butler of Tefton in Kent, Knight, and hath yffue by her now living, Spencer Fane, a fonne, and a daughter, named Anne Fane; Frances Fane, daughter to the faid deceafed lady, was married to Sir Robert Brett of Malling Abbey in Kent, Knight, but fhe deceafed before him, leaving no yffue furviving her. The officers of arms attended this funeral: the Counteffe of Weftmerland was chief mourner, fupported by the Earl Humes and the Lord Le Defpencer, affifted by my Lord's five daughters and Sir George Fane's lady, her trayne borne by the relict Lady Levefon; the affiftants to the corps were four of my Lord's youngeft fonnes; the great banner borne by Sir Henry Fane, Knight, cofferer to King Charles; the four banner-rolls carried by Sir George Fane, Sir Francis Wortley,

Wortley, Baronet, Sir Richard Levefon, Knight of the Bath, and Sir Warham St. Leger, Knight; the penon borne by Rowland Woodward, Efq; All which were offered up to the Earle of Weftmerland.

WESTMERLAND.

THOMAS HOWARD, Earl of SUFFOLK.

The Right Honourable THOMAS HOWARD, Earl of Suffolk and Baron of Walden, Knight of the moft noble order of the garter, and one of the lords of the king's majefty's moft honourable pryvye councel, departed this prefent life at Suffolk-houfe near Charing Crofs the xxviiith of Maye in the yeare of our Lord 1626. He was the fecond fonne of Thomas Duke of Norfolk, and of Margaret his fecond wife, daughter and only heire of Thomas Lord Audley of Walden. This honourable defunct maried Katharine, eldeft daughter and one of the heires of Sir Henry Knivett of Charlton in Wiltfhire, Knight, widow of Richard, eldeft fonne of Robert Lord Riche; by whom he had yffue, Theophilus, eldeft fonne, nowe Earle of Suffolk, and Lord Howard of Walden, who maried Lady Elizabeth, daughter and coheire of George Hume, Earle of Dunbarr; Thomas, 2d fonne, Earle of Berkfhire and Vifcount Andover, who maried Lady Elizabeth, daughter of William Earle of Excefter; Henry, 3d fonne, who maried Elizabeth, daughter and fole heire of Ralph Baffett of Blore, in the countye of Stafford, Efq; Sir Charles Howard, Knt. 4th fonne, who maried Mary, daughter and heire of Sir John Fitz of Devonfhire, and widow of Thomas Darcy, fonne and heire apparent of Thomas nowe Earle Rivers, Vifcount Colchefter and Baron Darcy of Chiche; before that having been the widow of Sir Allan Percye, Knight; Sir Robert Howard, 5th fonne, Knight of the Bathe at the creation of Prince Charles; Sir William Howard, 6th fonne, Knight of the Bath likewife at the creation of Prince Charles; Sir Edward Howard, 7th fonne, Knight of the Bath alfo at the creation of Prince Charles; Lady Elizabeth, eldeft daughter, maried to William Earle of Banburye; Lady Frances, 2d daughter, maried to Robert Earle of Somerfet; Lady Katharine, 3d daughter, maried to William Earle of Salifburye; Lady Margaret, 4th

daughter,

daughter, dyed younge, and was buried at Walden in Essex. This honourable defunct lyeth interred in the parish church of Walden in a vault under the chauncell. This certificate was taken by Thomas Preston, Portcullis, the second daye of Maye 1627.

FOULKE GREVILL, Lord BROOKE.

The Right Honourable Sir FOULKE GREVILL, Knight of the Bath, created by our late foveraigne lorde Kinge James Lord Brooke of Beauchamp's Court, in the countye of Warwick. Being defcended of an heire general of the auncient baronye of Willoughby Lord Brooke, he was fome tyme fervant in an honourable place to our late foveraigne lady Queene Elizabeth, after whofe death he was firft made Chauncellour of the Exchequer and Privye Counceller to our dread foveraigne lorde Kinge James, and one of the gentlemen of his majefty's bed-chamber: he was at the tyme of his death councellor of eftate to our moft dread foveraigne lorde King Charles that now is, and having attayned to the age of 74 yeres, departed this mortall life at Brooke-houfe in Holborne upon Tuefday the xxx[th] of September 1628, whofe body was mofte honourably convayed from thence to his caftle at Warwick, where his funerall was mofte nobly folempnized, according to his eftate, upon Monday the 27th of October following. He dyed a batchelor; his heire to the baronye was Robert Grevill Lorde Brooke, his uncle's grandchild, upon whom the faid baronye was eftated, who was principal mourner at the faid funeral, being then of the age of xxi years, and not maried. The executors of his laft will and teftament were the Right Honourable Sir John Coke, Knight, principal fecretarye of ftate, Sir Francis Swift, Knight, Mr. Michaell Mallett, and Mr. William Vyner. The officers of armes attended this funeral, by whom this certificate was taken, and verified by the fubfcription of

Jo: COKE.   MICH: MALLETT.
FRA: SWIFT.   WM VYNER.

ANTONY-MARIA BROWNE, Vifcount MOUNTAGUE.

The Right Honourable ANTONY-MARIA BROWNE, Vifcount Mountague, departed this mortall and tranfitorie life the 23d of October 1629, and was interred in the parifh church of Midhurft in Suffex by his aunceftors, the 27th of the faid month following. He maried JANE, daughter of the Right Honourable Thomas Sackvile, Earle of Dorfet and Lord High Treafurer of England; by whom he had yffue Francis Browne, nowe Vifcount Mountague, his fonne and heire, and fix daughters; Maria, eldeft daughter, maried to William Pawlet Lord St. John of Bafing, fonne and heire to the Marquis of Winchefter, after to William, 2d fonne of Thomas Lord Arundel of Wardour; Katharine, 2d daughter, maried to William Tirwhit of Kettleby, in the countie of Lincolne; Anne and Lucie, nunnes beyond feas; Frances, maried to John Blomer of the countie of Glocefter, Efquire; Marie, yongeft daughter, maried to Robert Petre, fonne and heire of the Lord Petre of Writtell in Effex. The executors of his laft will and teflament were Mr. Robert Petre, his fonne-in-law, and Mr. Thomas Arundell, fonne and heire to the Lord Arundell of Wardour. This certificate was taken by Sampfon Lennard, Blew Mantle.

GEORGE ABBOT, Arch Bifhop of CANTERBURY.

The mofte Reverend Father in God GEORGE ABBOT, late Arch Bifhop of Canterbury, primate of all England and metropolitan, was firft confecrated bifhopp of Coventrey and Litchfield, after tranflated to the fee of London; from whence, in the yeare 1611, he was by our late foveraigne Lord King James tranflated into the metropolitan fee of Canterbury, where he continued 22 yeares compleat, and was one of the mofte honourable privie councell to his facred majefty, and to our mofte gracious foveraigne that nowe is; and having attayned the yeares of 71, dyed at his pallace at Croydon on the 4th daye of Auguft, in the yeare of our Lord 1633, being never maried: whilft he lived, he beftowed much in pyous ufes, amongeft which he founded a fayre hofpitall and workhoufe for the poore at Guildford, where he was borne, endowing it with a revenew of 300 l. per annum. His funerals were most honourably folemnized at Croydon aforefaid on Tuefday the 3d of September following, and after the ceremony there ended, his grace's corpes was honourably conveyed to Guildford, attended with many of his friends and kindred in coaches. At Guildford the mayor, with his brethren, ftood in readinefs to receive him, and attended on his corpes to Trinity church, where he was interred. He made Sir Morris Abbott, Knt. citizen and alderman of London, his 5th brother, with Mr. Morris Abbott, 2d fonne of the faid Sir Morris, executors of his laft will and teftament, who performed all things in a mofte honourable and decent manner, according to the greatnefs and dignity of the place and offices he bore in the common wealth, etc. etc. Certified the 12 September 1633.

MORRIS ABBOTT.
GEO. ABBOTT.

ACCEPTED FREWEN, Arch Bifhop of YORK.

The moft Reverend Father in God ACCEPTED, Lord Arch Bifhop of York, primate of England, metropolitan, departed this mortall life at his houfe at Bifhop's Thorpe neare York (newly repaired at his great charge) on Monday the 28th of March 1664, in the 76th yeare of his age. He was made chaplaine in ordinary to his facred Majefty King Charles I. in the yeare 1625, and the yeare following was chofen prefident of Magdalen College in Oxford, whereof he was both pupill and fellow; and whilft he performed that charge with fingular prudence, he was made deane of Glocefter, and fower times vice-chancellor of that famous univerfity; and in the yeare 1644 he was confecrated bifhop of Coventry and Litchfield; but the fury of the late times prevented him in the adminiftration thereof, and retired him to a very ftrict folitude, till upon his majefty's moft happy returne to his government, he was tranflated to the fee of York on the 14th of November 1660. After his death his corps was privately removed to York, and there for divers dayes depofited in that decent ftate that was fuitable to the dignity of fo greate a prelate; and on Tuefday,

day the 3d of May was with all solemnity interred under the greate east w... of the cathedral church of St. Peter: the chief mourner was Mr. Stephen Frewen the sole executor and only-surviving brother of the defunct. The officers of arms attended this funeral, and the certificate here set forth was taken by Henry St. George, Esq; Richmond Herald, and attested by the said Mr. Stephen Frewen.

JAMES LEY, Earl of MARLEBOROUGH.

The Right Honourable and most noble Lord JAMES LEY, Earle of Marleborough, Baron Ley of Ley, sonne of Henry Earle of Marleborough, and grandchild of James first Earle of Marleborough, and Lord High Treasurer of England in the beginning of the reigne of the late King Charles, did from his youth apply himselfe to learned and generous studies, whereby he rendered himselfe highly capable to serve his prince and countrey; of which he gave signall testimony from the beginning of the late unhappy rebellion to the minute of his death, not onely by voluntarily exposing his person to all dangers, and valiantly fighting in his majesty's armyes; but in applying himselfe to navigation, wherein he became most expert, spending therein the greatest part of the last twenty yeares of his life, together with his patrimony, and in that time visited the American plantations and the West and East Indies, to the last of which he was sent by his majesty, anno 1662, with a fleet of ships and forces, to take possession of Bombaya in the East Indies, which, by agreement with the crown of Portugal, was then to be rendered to his majesty; in which charge he demeaned himselfe as became a man of honour and prudence. Lastly, this most noble Earle having the command of one of his majesty's principal ships of war, called the Old James, after he had rendered all possible proofes of his conduct and courage in the late naval battle against the Dutch, fought upon Saturday the 3d of June under the auspicious command of his Royal Highnes James Duke of York, he fell in the bed of honour, being slayne with a great shot, the like of which tooke away also, about halfe an hour before, the life of the Right Honourable and most noble Lord Charles Weston Earle of Portland, sonne of Jherom Earle

of

of Portland, and grandchild of Richard firſt Earle of Portland, who ſucceeded to this Earle's grandfather in the office of Lord High Treaſurer of England. This moſt noble Earle dyed unmarried in the 46th yeare of his age, and was buried near St. Edward's chapel in Weſtminſter Abbey with great ſolemnity; the particulars whereof are recorded in the Heralds Office with this certificate, which was taken by Sir Edward Walker, Knt. Garter principal king of arms, and atteſted by the Right Honourable Sir George Carteret, executor to the ſaid noble Earle defunct, the 20th daye of June 1665.

CHARLES BERKELEY, Earl of FALMOUTH.

The Right Honourable and moſt noble Lord CHARLES BERKELEY, Earle of Falmouth, Baron Botetourt of Langport in England, and Viſcount Fitzharding of Beerehaven, and Baron Berkeley of Rathdoune in Ireland, 2d ſonne of the Right Honourable Sir Charles Berkeley, Knt. (now Viſcount Fitzharding) Treaſurer of his majeſty's houſehold, and one of his majeſty's moſt honourable privy councell, did, in purſuance of his loyalty, even from his infancy, with all obſequiouſneſs apply himſelf unto the ſervice of his majeſty and the royall family, then forced to live in exile in foraigne parts, never forſaking them in the loweſt condition, but attending his Royall Highneſs the Duke of York in the armyes, both in France and Flanders, which induced his majeſty, ſince his happy reſtoration, to conferr thoſe honours upon him, as alſo to make him keeper of the privy purſe, and his Royall Highneſs to conſtitute him lieutenant-governor of Portſmouth, and captain of his horſe-guards.: hereupon, as an effect of gratitude and zeal to the ſervice of his majeſty and his royall highneſs, his lordſhip, ſome few dayes before the late engagement between the royall navy commanded by his royall highneſs and that of the Dutch, obtayned leave to goe on board his royall highneſs's ſhip, to be preſent and partaker in the danger ; where, in the naval battle fought upon Saturday the 3d of June, his lordſhip (being then very neare the perſon of his royall highneſs) was ſlayne with the ſame ſhot that alſo in the ſame moment deprived of life Charles Maccarty, Viſcount Muſkerry; and Richard Boyle, Eſq; 2d ſonne of Richard Earle of Burlington and Corke.

This

This moſt noble Earle married MARY, daughter of Colonel Harvey Bagot, Eſq; by whom he left iſſue the Lady Mary Berkeley, his ſole daughter and heire, being three weeks old at his death. As for his funeral, his majeſty (as an effect of the great favour and value he had for ſo meritorious a ſervant and ſubject) commanded that the ſame ſhould be ſolemnized at his majeſty's expence, which was moſt ſumptuouſly performed, the Lord Arch Biſhop of Canterbury, the Lord Chancellor, the Dukes of Monmouth and Ormond, and divers of the nobility of the three kingdoms attending, &c. &c. The corps were interred in a chapell on the north ſide of St. Edward's. This certificate was taken by Sir Edward Walker, Knt. Garter principal king of arms, and atteſted by the Right Honourable Charles Viſcount Fitzharding, father to the moſt noble Earle defunct, this 24th of June 1665.

ALGERNOUN PERCY, Earl of NORTHUMBERLAND.

The Right Honourable and moſt noble Lord ALGERNOUN PERCY, tenth Earle of Northumberland of that family, Baron Percy, Lucy, Poynings, Fitzpaine, Brian, and Latimer, one of the Lords of his majeſty's moſt honourable privy council, Lord Lieutenant of the countyes of Northumberland and Suſſex, and Knight of the moſt noble order of the garter, departed this mortall life in the 67th yeare of his age, at his honor of Petworth, in the countye of Suſſex, the 13th daye of October 1668, and was privately interred in a vault in the church of Petworth appropriated to his noble family, the 4th day of November following. This moſt noble Earle married two wives; the firſt was the Lady ANNE, eldeſt daughter of the Right Honourable William Earle of Saliſbury, &c. and Knight of the garter, by whom he had iſſue ſix daughters, two only living to be married; viz. the Lady Anne Percy, the eldeſt, was married unto Philip Lord Stanhope, Earle of Cheſterfield, and dyed without iſſue; the Lady Elizabeth, 2d daughter, is now wife of Arthur Lord Capell, Earle of Eſſex, by whom he hath iſſue the Lady Elizabeth Capell, about five yeares old. The ſecond wife of this moſt noble Earle is the Lady ELIZABETH HOWARD, daughter of Theophilus Earle of Suffolke, Knight of the garter, deceaſed, who ſurvives

H

vives him; by whom he had issue his only son Joceline, now Earle of Northumberland, &c. and Lord Lieutenant of the countyes of Northumberland and Sussex, who hath married the Lady Elizabeth Wriothesley, third daughter and coheire of Thomas Earle of Southampton, late Lord High Treasurer of England, &c. deceased, and sole heire of his second wife the Lady Elizabeth Leigh, who was daughter and coheire of Francis Lord Dunsmore, Earle of Chichester, deceased, by whom he hath issue the Lady Elizabeth Percy, aged about two yeares, as yet his only child. This certificate was taken the 29th daye of December 1668, by Sir Edward Walker, Knight, Garter principal king of arms, and attested by the subscription of the Right Honourable Joceline Earle of Northumberland, sonne and heire of the most noble Algernoun Earle of Northumberland, deceased.

Sir WILLIAM WILLUGHBY, Baronet.

The Right Worshipful Sir WILLIAM WILLUGHBY of Selston, in the county of Nottingham, Baronet, one of the Gentlemen of his majesty's privy chamber, as also one of his Deputy Lieutenants, and Captain of a troop of horse within the same county, departed this mortal life at his house called Selston-hall upon Fryday the tenth of February, a° 1670; whose funeral was honourably solemnized according to his degree on Thursday the 11th May next ensuing, from Selston-hall to the parish church of Selston, where he was interred on the south side of the chancel. He married MARGARET, daughter and sole heire to George Abbot, sonne and heire of Sir Morris Abbot, Knt. but left no issue by her then surviving; whereupon Mary, wife of Beaumont Dixey of Bosworth, in the county of Leicester, Esq; sonne and heire to Sir Wolston Dixey, Bart. (only sister to the defunct) became his lineal heire.

Sir FRANCIS CHAPLIN, Knight.

Sir FRANCIS CHAPLIN, Knt. late Lord Mayor of the city of London, and Alderman of Vintry Ward, one of the governors of Christ Hospital (to which

said

said hospital he bequeathed two hundred pounds by his last will and testament) departed this life at his house in Bery-street on Sunday the 27th day of June 1680, and was privately interred in the parish church of St. Catharine Cree on Saturday the 3d day of July following. The said Sir Francis Chaplin was eldest son of Sir Robert Chaplin of Bury St. Edmond's, in the county of Suffolk, and Elizabeth his wife, daughter of Francis Afty of Bury St. Edmond's aforesaid; which said Robert Chaplin, and Elizabeth his wife, left issue (besides the deceased) Robert Chaplin of the parish of St. Swithin, London, Merchant, his second son, who married Anne, eldest daughter of Sir Thomas Tomkins of Mornington, in the county of Hereford, Knight, and widow of Roger Vaughan of the county of Hereford aforesaid, Esq; The said Sir Francis Chaplin the defunct married ANNE, the daughter of Daniel Huett of Essex, Esq; by whom he left issue John Chaplin, his eldest son; Charles, 2d son; Robert, 3d son; and Anne, his only daughter. John Chaplin, Esq; son and heir of the defunct, married Elizabeth, the daughter and sole heir of Sir John Hamby of Tathwel, in the county of Lincoln, Knt. by his wife Elizabeth, daughter and sole heir of Richard Porter of Lamberhurst in Kent, Esq; by whom he hath issue three sons and one daughter; viz. Porter, eldest son; Francis, 2d son; and John, 3d son, and Anne his daughter. This certificate was taken the 23d of July 1683, by Henry St. George, Knt. Clarenceux king of arms, and attested by the subscription of Robert Chaplin, brother to the defunct.

ROB: CHAPLIN.

Sir EDWARD TURNOR, Knt. LORD CHIEF BARON, &c.

Sir EDWARD TURNOR, Knight, late Lord Chief Baron of his majesty's court of Exchequer, departed this life on the 4 day of March 1675, at the town and borough of Bedford, during the publick assizes there, being then one of the judges itinerant for the Norfolk circuit; from thence his body was privately removed to his house in Chancery-lane, London, where it remained till Thursday the 16 day of the said month; on which day it was with all due solemnity

lemnity befitting his degree conveyed through the city of London, accompanied with a great number of coaches, as the king's, queen's, their royal highnesses, the Arch Bishop of Canterbury's, the Lord Chancellor's, and divers of the nobility, relations, and others, as far as Kingsland juxta Newington, and proceeding thence to Hoddesdon in Hertfordshire, it was met by the principal gentry both of the counties of Hertford and Essex, who accompanied the corps to Little Parendon in Essex, where it was interred on the south side of the chancel of that parish church. He was eldest son of Arthur Turnor of Parendon Parva, Serjeant at law, by Anne his wife, daughter of John Jermy of Gunton, in the county of Norfolk, Esq; He was born near the Old Exchange, London, in the house of his uncle Sir Thomas Moulson, some time Lord Mayor of the said city; he was bred at school under Dr. Godwin, who writ the Roman Antiquities; from thence sent to Queen's College in Oxford under Dr. Barlow, now Bishop of Lincoln; from thence to the Middle Temple, where he studied the laws, until upon the king's restoration in the year 1660, he was made Knight, and one of the king's council in the law, and attorney-general to his royal highness: in the year 1661 he was chosen burgess for the town of Hertford to serve in that parliament, and then chosen Speaker thereof; and during the time of being Speaker he was made solicitor-general to his majesty, in the Easter-term 1671 made serjeant at law, and the same term was sworn Lord Chief Baron of his majesty's court of Exchequer, in which office he continued till his death. He married, firstly, Sarah, daughter and heir to Gerard Gore, Esq; Alderman of London, by whom he had issue four sons and two daughters; viz. Sir Edward Turnor, Knt. his eldest son, who married the Lady Isabella Keith, daughter and coheir of the Right Hon[ble] William Earl Marshal of Scotland, and by her hath had issue two sons, Charles, his son and heir, and Edward, who died an infant, and five daughters; Anne, Isabella, Sarah, Elizabeth, and Mary (whereof Sarah and Mary only survived): Arthur, 2d son, and Gerard, 3d son to the defunct, died infants; Arthur, 4th son, married Elizabeth, daughter of John Urlin of Eaton, in com. Berks, Esq; by whom he hath issue one son, named Edward. The daughters of the defunct are Sarah, married to George Clarke of Watford, in com. Northampton, Esq; the other, named Anne, died an infant.

The

The second wife to the defunct was MARY, daughter and heir of Henry Ewer of South Mimms, in com. Midx. Gent. widow of William Afhton of Tingreth, in com. Bedford, Efq; but by her he hath had no iffue.

The officers of arms who marfhalled this funeral were Henry St. George, Efq; Richmond Herald, and Robert Devenifh, Efq; York Herald; and the truth of this certificate is attefted by the before-mentioned Sir Edward Turnor, Knt. fon and heir to the defunct, the fixth day of March 1682, annoq; R. R. Caroli Secundi, nunc Angliæ, etc. 35°.

I muft here beg the Reader's excufe, if I have too long detained him with fo many examples of the fame kind, of which we have many volumes finely preferved on vellum; but as fuch monumental pedigrees have not hitherto been publifhed, and as the fame tend fo much to the honour and prefervation of the memory of families, I hope they are not improperly introduced here, becaufe fuch Funeral Certificates muft ever be held in veneration, not only for the Genealogies they contain, but alfo for the great ufe and advantages that may arife from them to the public in general in various other inftances: to the Hiftorian they may be of excellent fervice to affift him in the chronology of remarkable tranfactions at home or abroad, in peace or war; the feveral fteps to preferment in church or ftate; where family alliances principally lie are thereby known; and a multitude of difcoveries made, which may give lights into the changes and proceedings of government, &c. are abundant proofs of their value and ufe to pofterity.

I

But to resume the subject of Parish Registers, I shall here beg leave to present the reader with a few examples of certificates lately registered in the HERALDS OFFICE, in support of pedigrees for families residing abroad, which will shew the exactness and attention that is generally paid to these affairs by other nations.

From the pedigree of Baron QUARLES, Lord of Tedingsweerd in Guelderland, &c.

"JEAN QUARLES, bachelier, né à Londres, demeure à Delft avec PETRO-
"NELLA VAN BERCHELL, demoiselle de Rotterdam, ayant eu leur trois an-
"nonces de marriages sans aucun empechement legitime, sont publiquement
"dans l'eglise de Rotterdam investi dans le saint etat de marriage le 31 Octobre
"1628.

JOHANNES WILHELMINS,
Eccleti: Rottrod:"

Extrait du Regiftre de baptesmes de l'eglise Walonne de Voorburg.

"Le 22 Janvier 1760 est née HENRIETTE PHILIPPINE WILHELMINE
"FREDERIQUE, fille de Monsieur le Baron Guillaume de Quarles, Seigneur
"de Thedingsweerd, et de Madame la Baronne Louise Henriette de Wyhe
"d'Egtel son epouse: elle a été presentée au baptesme le 3 Fevrier 1760 par
"Monsieur son pere et par Madame la Baronne de Heckeren de Camperbeke,
"née Baronne de Wyhe, qui en est maraine.

"Fait à Voorburg le 26 May 1763.

J. J. CUSSY, Pasteur."

"Pro vero Extr.

[31]

From the continuation of the family pedigree of ACTON, of Besançon in France, descended from the ancient ACTONS of Aldenham, &c. in the county of Salop.

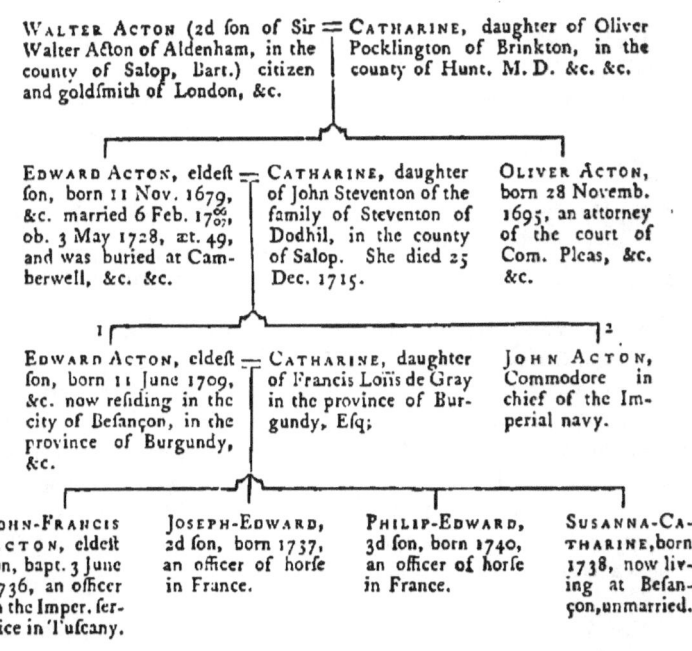

WALTER ACTON (2d son of Sir = CATHARINE, daughter of Oliver
Walter Acton of Aldenham, in the | Pocklington of Brinkton, in the
county of Salop, Bart.) citizen | county of Hunt. M. D. &c. &c.
and goldsmith of London, &c.

EDWARD ACTON, eldest = CATHARINE, daughter OLIVER ACTON,
son, born 11 Nov. 1679, | of John Steventon of the born 28 Novemb.
&c. married 6 Feb. 17⁰⁶/₀₇, | family of Steventon of 1695, an attorney
ob. 3 May 1728, æt. 49, | Dodhil, in the county of the court of
and was buried at Cam- | of Salop. She died 25 Com. Pleas, &c.
berwell, &c. &c. | Dec. 1715. &c.

EDWARD ACTON, eldest = CATHARINE, daughter JOHN ACTON,
son, born 11 June 1709, | of Francis Loüis de Gray Commodore in
&c. now residing in the | in the province of Bur- chief of the Im-
city of Besançon, in the | gundy, Esq; perial navy.
province of Burgundy,
&c.

JOHN-FRANCIS   JOSEPH-EDWARD,   PHILIP-EDWARD,   SUSANNA-CA-
ACTON, eldest   2d son, born 1737, 3d son, born 1740, THARINE, born
son, bapt. 3 June an officer of horse an officer of horse 1738, now liv-
1736, an officer in France.   in France.   ing at Besan-
in the Imper. ser-   çon, unmarried.
vice in Tuscany.

OLIVER ACTON, Gent. an attorney in the court of Common Pleas, and steward of the hospital of Bridewell, London (the same Oliver Acton above-mentioned) by his affidavit, and authentic evidences which are entered in the Heralds Office, prove the former part of this pedigree, and the certificates

from

from the Register abroad the latter. That for JOHN-FRANCIS ACTON, the eldest son, is as follows:

Extrait des Registres de la paroisse de St. Marcellin de Besançon.

"JEAN FRANÇOIS EDOÜARD, fils de Monsieur Edouard Acton, Gentilhomme Anglois, et de Madame Catharine Loïs son epouse, a été baptisé le trois Juin Mil sept cent trente six : il a eu pour parrein Monsieur Jean Etienne Caboud, Lieutenant-General du bailliage de Besançon, et pour marreine Madame Françoise d'Osson."

"Certifie le present extrait conforme à l'original : à Besançon 10 May 1762.

D. GEORGE COUDERET, Ret. Ben.
Curé de St. Marcellin."

"Nous ANTOINE FRANÇOIS DES POTOTS, Ecuyer, President au presidial, Lieutenant-General au bailliage de Besançon au comté de Bourgoyne, où le papier timbré n'est pas en usage, certifions à tous à qui il apartiendra, que Dom. George Couderet, qui a signé l'extrait baptistaire cy-desus, est religieux Benedictin Curé de la paroisse de St. Marcellin de cette ville, et que soy pleine et entiere y doit estre ajoutée comme à tous autres actes qu'il signe en cette qualitée ; en temoignage de quoy nous avons signé les presentes, et y avons aposé le sceau du roy, dont on se sert en ce bailliage. Donné en nostre hotel à Besançon le onze May Mil sept cent soixante deux."

"Nous Vicaire-General de son eminence Monseigneur le Cardinal de Choiseul Beaupré, Archeveque de Besançon, Prince du St. Empire, certifions à qui il appartiendra, que Dom. Couderet, qui a ecrit, signé, et delivré l'acte d'autre part inseré, est tel qu'il se qualifie ; que foy pleine et entiere doit y être ajoutée tant en jugement que de hors, certifions en outre, que le papier timbré n'est point en usage au comté de Bourgoyne. A Besançon le onze May Mil sept cent soixante deux.

GALOIS, Vic. Ger.

"Par M. le Vicaire-General JOLICARS."

Part of the pedigree of Sir JOHN LAMBERT, Bart.

Sir JOHN LAMBERT, Knt. born anno 1666, created a baronet of Great Britain by letters patent 16 Feb. 1710, 9° Annæ Reginæ: he died Feb. 4, 1722. = MADELAIN, daughter of Benjamin Beauzelin, of Roan in Normandy: she died in Clarges-ftreet, Piccadilly, 1737, æt. 70.

Sir JOHN LAMBERT of the parifh of St. Peter le Poor, London, Baronet. = ANNE, daughter of Tempeft Holmes, Efq; late one of the commiffioners of his majefty's victualling office, living at Paris, 1762.

BENJAMIN LAMBERT of London, Efquire.

Sir JOHN LAMBERT, baptiz'd in the parifh church of Saint Peter le Poor, London, Oct. 11, 1728, living 1762.

ROBERT ALEXANDER LAMBERT, 2d fon, born at Paris, and baptized there 24th July 1732, living 1762.

BENJAMIN LIDDEL LAMBERT, 3d fon, born at Paris 6 Aug. and baptized 20th of faid month 1735.

BERKELEY FITZWILLIAMS LAMBERT, 4th fon, born at Paris, and baptized there the 11th Jan. 1738 N.S.

Proofs of the births of the three fons born at Paris; viz.

The baptifm of ROBERT ALEXANDER, 2d fon of Sir John Lambert, and Lady Anne Holmes his wife, is certified by the Rev. Anthony Thompfon, chaplain to his excellency the late Earl of Waldegrave, then charged with his late majefty's affairs at the court of France, with thefe particulars, that Robert Knight, Efq; and Mr. Alexander Alexander, were the godfathers, and Mrs. Knight, godmother.

K   Certificate

Certificate for BENJAMIN LIDDEL LAMBERT the third son.

IMMANUEL!

Extrait des Regiſtres des Bâtemes de ceux de la confeſſion d'Augſbourg, que font leurs aſſemblées ſacrées ches Monſieur le Miniſtre Plenipotentiare de Suede.

" Vendredi le 20ᵐᵉ Août, à 7 heures du ſoir, de l'année 1736, en l'hotel et
" à la chapelle de Monſieur le Baron de Gedda, Miniſtre Plenipotentiare de
" Suede, dans la ruë des Sts. Peres, fauxbourg St. Germain à Paris, fut baptiſé
" un fils de Monſieur Jean Lambert, Chevailler Baronet de la Grande Britagne,
" de Dame Anne Holmes Lambert ſon epouſe; les parains etoient le Sieur Ben-
" jamin Lambert, Ecuier de Londres, abſent, repreſenté par le dit Chevalier
" Jean Lambert ſon frere; le ſecond parain le Reverend Charles Liddel, Anglois,
" curé de la paroiſſe de ...... dans la province de Kent, auſſi abſent, et repre-
" ſenté par le Docteur en Medecine Lane, Anglois; et la maraine Demoiſelle
" Sara Parſons, fille ainée de Monſieur Humphrey Parſons, Alderman de la ville
" de Londres, et Membre du parlement pour la dite ville; lesquels parains et
" maraine ont donné à l'enfant le nom BENJAMIN LIDDEL: l'enfant fut né
" Lundi le 6ᵐᵉ Août 1736, à trois heures du matin.

" Fait à Paris le 26   DANIEL LOUIS METTENIUS, Miniſtre du ſaint
" Octobre 1736."   Evangile, et Predicateur de la legation de
                            Suede, certifie que le preſent extrait eſt con-
                            forme à ſon original.

" Je certifie que l'extrait baptiſtaire de l'autre part eſt de l'aumonier de la le-
" gation veritable qui il a ſigné, et qno'n y peut ajouter pleine foy. Fait à Paris
" le 17 Oct. 1736.
                    Min. Plenipot. du roy de Suede à la cour de France."

Certificate

Certificate for BERKELEY FITZ-WILLIAMS LAMBERT,
fourth son.

"I the under-written chaplain to his excellency the Earl of Waldegrave, his majesty's ambassador extraordinary and plenipotentiary at the court of France, do hereby certify, that according to the form required by the church of England, and before several witnesses, I baptized BERKELEY FITZ-WIL-LIAMS, the new-born son of Sir John Lambert and Lady Anne Lambert his wife, the eleventh day of January in the year of our Lord One thousand Seven hundred and thirty-eight.

ANT. THOMPSON.

N. B. The Earls of Berkeley and Fitz-Williams were godfathers, and the Lady Wolseley, wife of Sir William Wolseley of Wolseley Bridge, in the county of Stafford, Baronet, godmother.

And from the family pedigree of the Chevalier DE LÉRY, Knight of the order of St. Louis; among several other certificates entered in the HERALDS OFFICE as proofs of that pedigree, please to observe the following:

Extrait des Regiſtres des Baptêmes de la paroiſſe de Ville Marie en l'iſle de Montreal en Canada.

"Le cinquieme jour d'Octobre de l'an Mil six cent quatre vingt dix sept a été baptizé MARIE RENEE, fille de Renée de Gardeur, Ecuyer, Sieur de Bauvais, Lieutenant dans le detachement de la marine, et de Dame Marie Barbe de St. Our son epouse, née le meme jour des dits mois et an: le parrein a été Jean Batiste de St. Our, et la marraine Genevieve Marjane de la Valterie, femme de Mr. L'Iſle, Ecuyer et Lieutenant dans le dit detachement. Signé, "DE L'ESCHAILLON, GENEVIEVE DE LA VALTERIE, R. C. DE BRESLAY, faiſant les fonctions Curiales."

"Je

" Je fous-figné, Pretre Vicaire de la dite paroiffe de Ville Marie, certifie que
" le prefent extrait eft veritable et conforme à fon original.   Expedie ce 4 Juil-
" let 1715.

PRIAT, Vicaire."

Extrait des Regiftres de la paroiffe de Quebec pour les Ba-
têmes, Marriages, et Enterrement, fait en 1721.

" Le vingt et unieme Juillet Mil fept cent et un, par nous Pretre fous-figné a
" été baptifé GASPARD JOSEPH, né le jour precedent du legitime marriage de
" Gafpar Chauffegros, Ecuyer, Sieur de Lery, Capitaine Ingenieur, et de Dame
" Marie René Legardeur de Bauvais; paraine Alexandre Jofeph de Leftimgand,
" Ecuyer, Sieur de St. Martin, Capitaine Commandant de les troupes en ce païs;
" maraine Dame Louife Legardeur, veuve de Monfieur de Villeray.

Signé au Regiftre, CHAUSSEGROS de Lery,
DE LESTIMGAND de St. Martin,
LOUISE LEGARDEUR de Villeray Bouillard.

" Nous Pretre Curé de Quebec certiffions le prefent extrait veritable et con-
" forme à l'original; en foy dequoy nous l'avons figné au dit Quebec le vingt
" deux Octobre Mil fept cent cinquante et un.

J. F. RECHES, Curé de Quebec.

" Nous Henric Marie du Breil de Pombriand, par la mifericorde de Dieu et
" la grace du St. Siege Apoftoloique Eveque de Quebec, fuffragant immediat du
" St. Seige, Confeiller du roy en tous fes confeils, etc. certifions à qui il appar-
" tiendra, que la fignature de l'extrait de l'autre part eft veritablement du Sr
" Rechés, Curé de Quebec, et que foy peut et doit y être ajouté. Donné à
" Quebec en notre palais epifcopal fous notre feing, le fceau de nos armes, et
" le contre-feing de notre fecretaire, ce 26 Octobre Mil fept cent cinquante un.

H. M. Eveque de Quebec."

To this is added a similar certificate, signed by the Chevalier François Bigot, Intendant of all New France.

Extrait du Regiftre de Bapt. faits à l'eglife paroiffe de St. Euftache à Paris.

"1762, le Vendredi 15 Octobre fut baptifé Louis René, né de Mercredi, dernier fils de Meffire Jofeph Gafpard Chauffegros, Ecuyer, Sieur de Lery, Chevalier de St. Louis, Capitaine dans les troupes du Roy cy devant en Canada, et de Dame Louife Martelle de Brouague fon epoufe, demeurants en rue du Boulloir; le parein Meffire Jean Louis la Corne, Pretre du diocefe de Canada; la maraine Renée de la Valliere, epoufe de Monf. Dulinot, Confeiller du cy devant grand voyer en Canada; lefquels ont figné."

"Collationé à l'original et delivré par moi Pretre Bachelier en theologie de faculté de Paris, Predicateur ordinaire du roy, et Vicaire de la dite eglife.

"A Paris ce 25 Octobre 1762. FRESNEAU."

The General Regiftry of BIRTHS eftablifhed in the HERALDS OFFICE, calculated to comprehend the numerous births of perfons not baptized in the eftablifhed church, is certainly a good one, and will be of great ufe in clearing up many difficulties with regard to INHERITANCES and CLAIMS of different natures; but as this is not known, perhaps, fo generally as it might be, I fhall, for the fake of all perfons, whether natives or foreigners, whom the extenfive commerce of this nation may invite to live among us, give them the following PLAN, eftablifhed in the year 1747, which I prefume will not be unacceptable.

A GENERAL

REGISTRY OF BIRTHS,

KEPT AT

The HERALDS OFFICE,

On St. Benet's Hill near St. Paul's, LONDON.

THE supreme Courts of judicature being held near this metropolis, a GENERAL REGISTRY of BIRTHS from all parts of his majesty's dominions collected into one, and ready at hand to be consulted, as in the case of Wills, must save great trouble and expence, which people are put to when it is necessary to consult such Registers as are now kept dispersed in the several parishes, and which do not comprehend the numerous births of children not baptized in the established church, or not baptized at all.

Proper books are provided for making the necessary entries; viz. for LONDON, and Places within the BILLS of MORTALITY; for the COUNTRY; and for the COLONIES abroad: likewise one for entering the births of persons of any age born before Christmas-day 1747.

There

[39]

There is daily attendance given, Holidays excepted, at the COLLEGE OF ARMS, or HERALDS OFFICE aforesaid, at the usual office-hours; viz. from Ten in the morning till One, and from Three till Five in the afternoon, by an Herald and a Pursuivant, who are sworn officers; one of whom will make due and exact entries of what is brought before them.

For such who live in London, and can conveniently come to the office, one or both the Parents are desired to attend there in person; or, in case that cannot be done, two persons who were present at the birth; the Midwife for one, if convenient, may attend and sign the entry, which is witnessed by two Officers of Arms in the Register-book, on paying the fee of Half a Crown; and at the same time an attested certificate of the entry made is given upon parchment, and sealed with the seal of the office.

For persons at a distance, they are desired to draw up a certificate, to be signed either by one or both the Parents, or by two persons present at the birth, and, if convenient, the Midwife for one; and to go to some neighbouring Justice of the peace, before whom they are desired to make affidavit of the truth; which certificate and affidavit being transmitted to the Office, with the Fee of Half a Crown, will be duly entered by one of the officers in waiting, and the originals be carefully kept: but if one person present at the birth can attend the

Office,

Office, and bring a certificate signed by one or both the Parents, or two persons present at the birth, done in his presence, such certificate will be entered, the person so attending signing the entry in the Register-book in the presence of one of the officers in waiting.

The time and place of the Parents Marriage is also given in, because it may be a means of proving those marriages with more ease; and the NAME of the Mother's Father must always be inserted.

The form of an ENTRY when both Parents sign.

Our ⟨Son JOHN / Daughter ANNE⟩ was born at our ⟨House / Lodgings⟩ in the Parish of ⟨St. John, / Hatfield,⟩ in the ⟨County of Essex, / City of London,⟩ on the fourth day of June, in the year One thousand seven hundred and forty-one; we having been married at St. Bride's in London on the third day of May, in the year 1740; as witness our hands this 6th of Jan. 1747.

RICHARD DOE,

Son of John Doe, by Anne his wife, daughter of Tho. Stiles.

MARY DOE,

Daughter of John Roe, of ⟨St. Luke's / Ham⟩ in the ⟨City of York. / County of Essex.⟩

Witnesses present at the birth of John Doe on June 4, 1741, as above,

A. B. Midwife. C. D. Nurse.

The form of an ENTRY when only one Parent signs.

My ^(Son JOHN,)_(Daughter ANNE,) by Mary my wife, daughter of John Roe of St. Luke's, ^(Ham,) in the ^(City of York,)_(County of Essex,) to whom I was married at St. Bride's in London on the third day of May, in the year 1740, was born at my ^(Lodgings)_(House) in the parish of ^(Hatfield,)_(St. John,) in the ^(County of Essex,)_(City of London,) on the fourth day of June, in the year One thousand seven hundred and forty-one; as witness my hand this 6th Jan. 1747.

Witnesses present at the birth of John Doe on June 4, 1741, as above,
A. B. Midwife,
C. D. Nurse.

RICHARD DOE,
Son of John Doe, by Anne his wife, daughter of Tho. Stiles.

The form of an ENTRY when Parents are dead, or cannot attend, and the Marriages cannot be known.

^(JOHN,)_(ANNE,) the ^(Son)_(Daughter) of Richard Doe by Mary his wife, daughter of John Roe of ^(St. Luke's,)_(Ham,) in the ^(City of York,)_(County of Essex,) was born at his father's ^(House)_(Lodgings) in the parish of ^(St. John,)_(Hatfield,) in the ^(City of London,)_(County of Essex,) on the fourth day of June, in the year One thousand seven hundred and forty-one; at which birth we were present, and do certify that the said Richard and Mary Doe did stile themselves man and wife, did cohabit, and were reputed as such for at least nine months before this child was born; as witness our hands this 6th Jan. 1747.

A. B. Midwife, C. D. Nurse,
And others present.

[42]

And as a matter further concerning the prefent fubject, I fhall here introduce a fhort Genealogical Table of feigned Names as a fpecimen, to fhew the manner of Regiftering Pedigrees in the HERALDS OFFICE at this time; viz.

A.

MARY, 2d daughter of Roger Caine of Cromwell, in the county of Midx. Efq; born 12 June 1678 at Cromwell, and there married the 20 Oct. 1699. She died the 15 Sept. following at Oldburn, and was buried in the chancel of that church.
1ft wife.

B.

JOHN HERALD of Oldburn, in the county of Northumberland, Efq; (2d fon of Sir John Herald of Rowland, in the county of Leicefter, Knt.) born at Rowland 14 May 1680, knighted at Whitehall 20th Aug. 1704: he was afterwards a colonel of a regiment of foot, and governor of the town and garrifon of Berwick upon Tweed, where he died 20 May 1728, and was buried in the fouth ifle of that church.

C.

MARY, eldeft daughter of Roger Watfon of Nutwood, in the county of Northumb. Gent. born at Nutwood 15 Aug. 1682, and there married 10 Oct. 1701. She died the 20 June 1710, in the parifh of St. Martin's in the Fields, Weftminfter, and was buried in the chancel of that church.
2d wife.

JAMES HERALD, Efq; eldeft fon, born at Oldburn 14 Sept. 1700: he was a lieutenant in the Hon. Col. John Kemp's regiment of foot in Ireland, where he died unmarried 28 Nov. 1736, and was buried in St. Patrick's church, Dublin.

JOHN HERALD, D. D. 2d fon, born at Oldburn 12 April 1703: mafter of Chrift's college, Camb. rector of Taufield, and alfo of Donmoor in Effex, and prebend of Lincoln. He died 28 Dec. 1759, and was buried in the church of Donmoor aforefaid.

JANE, 2d daughter and coheir of Robert Dore of Highwick, in the county of Berks, Efq; She was born at Highwick 20 June 1704; married at Acton in Berks 29 June 1724, now living, 1764.

CHRISTMAS, only daughter, born at Berwick the 25 Dec. 1705; married the 30 Nov. 1725 at St. Andrew's Holborn, to Geo. Errington of Gray's Inn, Efq; by whom fhe has iffue.

JOHN HERALD, of Highwick, Efq; eldeft fon, born at Donmoor aforefaid, June 11, 1725; a cornet of a regiment of dragoons; living, 1764, in Ireland unmarried.

JAMES HERALD, 2d fon, born in the parifh of St. Andrew Holborn, 12 July 1726; an officer in the Eaft India company's fervice at Fort St. David; living there 1762 unmarried.

ROBERT HERALD, 3d fon, born in the parifh of Slycomb in Berks, Sept. 14, 1727; was captain of a man of war. He died at Plymouth unmarried 19 June 1762, and was there buried.

THOMAS HERALD, 4th fon, born in the parifh of St. Margaret Weftminfter, 4 Oct. 1728. Member of parliament for the town of Bowland in Yorkfhire; living, 1764, unmarried.

ANNA-MARIA, only daughter, born at Pancras, in Midx. 3 Dec. 1730, and died at Bath 14 Dec. 1760 unmarried, and was buried in that cathedral.

See the Anceftors of Sir JOHN HERALD and his two wives, p. 50.

And

The truth of such a pedigree must be properly certified by one of the family; and to make it still more valid, with entries of extracts from parish regifters, wills, or monumental infcriptions, &c. And if a pedigree should be carried higher than this, or begin before the time that parish regifters commenced, an affidavit is not only required, but there must be recourfe to wills as aforefaid, deeds, or marriage fettlements, to corroborate the fame: fuch or the like proofs, concerning the refpective marriages, births, baptifms, deaths, and places of burial, as I shall prefently introduce, will, I hope, convince every unprejudiced and impartial perfon, that Pedigrees thus entered in the Heralds Office, fo well fortified, will be deemed hereafter, in cafes of affinity and confanguinity, very conclufive; but in cafe a century hence fuch a pedigree should be doubted, or the particulars intimated shall not be thought fufficient to fupport it, go to the war-office, and you will find Sir John Herald the colonel, his eldeft fon, James the lieutenant, and his grandfon John the cornet, in the books there. Examine the feveral parochial regifters, and if properly kept, or not deftroyed, you will there find the feveral entries. Go to Chrift's College, Cambridge, &c. and you will there find John Herald, D. D. examine the matriculation books, and you will alfo find him there proved to be the fon of Sir John Herald the colonel: go to Gray's Inn, and there perhaps you will find George Errington, a bencher. And if you want a further proof of the exiftence of the grandchildren of Sir John Herald

[44]

Herald aforesaid, examine the respective registers; and if it should be wanted to discover the death of James, one of the grandsons, who was in the East Indies, and unmarried in the year 1762, examine the East India company's books, and there, according to their wonted exactness and obliging behaviour, you will obtain a very particular account of him. Robert, the third grandson, will be found upon record in the admiralty-office; and Thomas the fourth grandson, the member of parliament, will be found upon that honourable list; and ANNA-MARIA, the grand-daughter, said to have died unmarried, will appear by an inscription in the cathedral at Bath; but in case the inscription should be defaced or worn out, see the Heralds Collections of monumental Inscriptions in the Heralds Office, and there you will find an exact copy preserved, as follows:

Here resteth the body of
ANNA-MARIA,
only daughter of the Rev: JOHN HERALD, D. D.
late Master of Christ's College, Cambridge, and Prebend of Lincoln, &c.
by JANE his wife, 2d daughter and coheir of ROBERT DORE,
of Highwick in the county of Berks, Esq;
and grand-daughter of Sir JOHN HERALD, Knt.
She died in this city unmarried the 14th of Dec: 1760,
aged 30 years.

Her eldest brother JOHN HERALD of Highwick aforesaid, Esq;
by whom she was much beloved, caused this memorial of her
to be placed here,
Anno 1764.

Select

Select Extracts of the REGISTERS of sundry Parishes, with Copies of Monumental Inscriptions, concerning the upper part of the Pedigree of Sir JOHN HERALD, Knt. aforesaid, as follow:

MARRIAGES.

WHITBY Register, YORKSHIRE.

HERALD, and BILAND. — Sir JOHN (eld. son of Rich. Herald of York, Esq;) of Rowland in com. Leicester, Knt. B. and JANE, eld. dau. of Sir James Biland of this town, Knt. S. were married by lycence.   1672 May 10.

ST. JOHN's Register, NEWCASTLE UPON TYNE.

CAINE, and FENWICK. — ROGER (2d son of Ralph Caine of Exeter, Gent.) of Cromwell in com. Midx. Esq; B. and ELIZABETH, 3d daughter of Thomas Fenwick of Oldburn in Northumb. S. were married by banns.   1673 June 12.

GREENWOOD Register, NORTHUMBERLAND.

WATSON, and SELBY, rel. of Hall. — ROGER (only son of Charles Watson of Carlisle, M. D.) of Nutwood in this county, Gent. B. and SARAH, 3d daughter of John Selby, and relict of Roger Hall, both of Newby in this parish, Esquires, were married by lycence.   1678 July 14.

CROMWELL Register, MIDDLESEX.

HERALD, and CAINE. — JOHN (2d son of Sir John Herald of Rowland, in com. Leic. Knt.) of Oldburn in com. Northumb. Esq; B. and MARY, 2d da. of Roger Caine of this parish, Esq; S. were married by banns.   1699 Oct. 20.

Nutwood Register, Northumberland.

HERALD, and WATSON.	JOHN (2d son of Sir John Herald of Rowland, in com. Leic. Knt.) of Oldburn in com. Northumb. Esq; W. and MARY, eld. da. of Roger Watson of this parish, S. were married by banns.	1701 Oct. 10.

BIRTHS and BAPTISMS.

Cromwell Register, Middlesex.

		Baptisms.
CAINE.	MARY, 2d daughter of Roger Caine of this parish, Esq; and Elizabeth his wife (3d daughter of Thomas Fenwick of Oldburn, in com. Northumb.) was born 12 June, and bapt. the twenty-eighth of said month.	1678 June 28.

Rowland Register, Leicestershire.

HERALD.	JOHN, 2d son of Sir John Herald of this parish, and Jane his wife (eldest dau. of Sir James Biland of Whitby, Knt.) was born 14 May, and baptized the second of next month following.	1680 June 2.

Nutwood Register, Northumberland.

WATSON.	MARY, daughter of Roger Watson of this parish, Gent. and Sarah his wife (3d daughter of John Selby of Newby, in the parish of Greenwood, Esq; and relict of Roger Hall of Newby aforesaid, Esq;) was born 15 August, and bapt. the first of September following.	1682 Sept. 1.

Oldburn Register, Northumberland.

HERALD.	JAMES, the only son of John Herald of this parish, Esq; and Mary his wife (2d dau. of Roger Caine of Cromwell in Midx. Esq;) was born 14 Sept. and baptized the fourteenth of next month following.	1700 Oct. 14.

HERALD. JOHN, fon of John Herald of this parifh, Efq; by Mary   1703
his 2d wife (eldeft dau. of Roger Watfon of Nutwood   May 9.
in this county, Gent.) was born 12 April, and bapt.
the ninth of next month following.

BERWICK Regifter.

HERALD. CHRISTMAS, only daughter of Sir John Herald, Knt.   1705
governor of this town, and Mary his 2d wife (eldeft   Dec. 25.
dau. of Roger Watfon of Nutwood, in com. Northum.
Gent.) was born and baptized on Chriftmas-day.

DEATHS and BURIALS.

OLDBURN Regifter, NORTHUMBERLAND.

Burials.

HERALD. MARY, the wife of John Herald of this parifh, Efq;   1700
(2d dau. of Roger Caine of Cromwell, in com. Midx.   Sept. 20.
Efq,) died 15 Sept. and was buried the twentieth.

ST. MARTIN'S IN THE FIELDS Regifter, WESTMINSTER.

HERALD. MARY, 2d wife of Sir John Herald of Oldburn, in   1710
com. Northum. Knt. (eldeft dau. of Roger Watfon of   June 25.
Nutwood, in faid county, Gent.) died 20 June, and
was buried the twenty-fifth following.

BERWICK Regifter.

HERALD. Sir JOHN HERALD of Oldburn, in com. Northumb.   1728
Knt. colonel of a regiment of foot, and governor of   May 23.
this town (2d fon of Sir John Herald) died 20 May,
and was buried the twenty-third following.

St. Patrick's Register, Dublin.

HERALD. JAMES HERALD, Esq; (eldest son of Sir John Herald, Knt. late governor of Berwick upon Tweed) died the 28th day of November, and was buried the third of next month following in the north isle.   1730 Dec. 3.

Donmoore Register, Essex.

HERALD. The Rev. JOHN HERALD, D. D. (2d son of Sir John Herald, Knt.) master of Christ's college, Camb. rector of this church, and prebend of Lincoln, &c. died the 28th day of December last, and was buried this second of January following.   1760 Jan. 2.

MONUMENTAL INSCRIPTIONS.

In the chancel of Oldburn church in Northumberland.

Here lieth the body of
M A R Y,
wife of JOHN HERALD of this parish, Esq;
2d daughter of ROGER CAINE of Cromwell,
in the county of Middlesex, Esq;
by ELIZABETH his wife, 3d daughter of THOMAS FENWICK, Esq;
lord of this manor.
She died the 15th day of September 1700,
aged 22 years.

She left issue JAMES, her only son,
who was born the day before his mother died.

In the chancel of St. Martin in the Fields, Weftminfter.

> To the memory of
> Dame MARY,
> 2d wife of Sir JOHN HERALD of Oldburn,
> in the county of Northumberland, Knt.
> eldeft daughter of ROGER WATSON of Nutwood, in the faid county, Gent.
> by SARAH his wife, 3d daughter of JOHN SELBY, and relict of ROGER HALL,
> both of Newby in the faid county, Efquires.
> She departed this life the 20th day of June 1710,
> in the 28th year of her age,
> leaving iffue JOHN, her only fon, born the 12th day of April 1703, and
> CHRISTMAS, her only daughter, born the 25th day of December 1705.

Entries from Parifh Regifters, or Copies of monumental Infcriptions as here fet forth, when entered with pedigrees in the Heralds Office, will anfwer the feveral purpofes required; but if pedigrees with fuch particulars are not entered in the Heralds Office, how will pofterity be able to deduce the courfe of inheritance? not eafily from Church Regifters or Wills, though they are ever fo well kept or preferved, becaufe they are difperfed in fo many, perhaps obfcure, places in this kingdom, and fo widely diftant from one another. It is therefore evident, from the frequent inftances of the difficulties, trouble, and great expence of obtaining a certain knowledge of wills, and of the places where people have been born, married, buried, or regiftered, whether in the eftablifhed church or otherwife, that it is highly neceffary, not only for the head or principal

[50]

cipal of every family, but also the younger sons or daughters, carefully to maintain the proofs of their descent, as the succession to estates, titles, &c. after long intermission of time, by the extinction of the former, may happen to revive in the latter.

In the pedigree represented in page 42, beginning with Sir JOHN HERALD and his two wives, neither Sir John's, nor his wives mothers names are mentioned; but if the Reader is curious to trace and discover who they were, let him examine the three first Registers of MARRIAGES and the three first of BIRTHS and BAPTISMS, in p. 45, 46, and there he will find them, and the two last Inscriptions to confirm the same, in the following manner:—

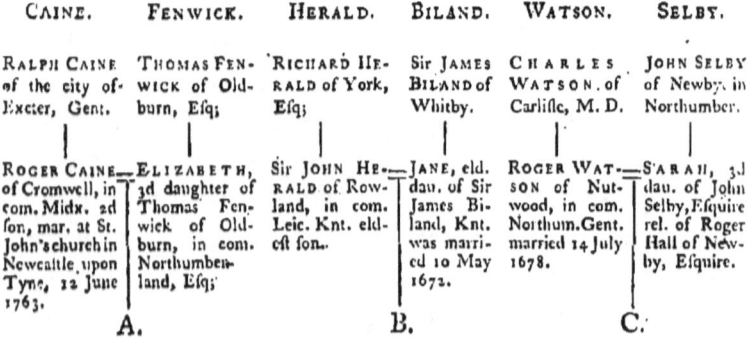

Having

Having thus far confidered the different methods of preferving a remembrance of families, and having particularly fhewn the manner of regiftering pedigrees in the HERALDS OFFICE, it may not be amifs to obferve, that the OFFICE is a BODY CORPORATE, acting under a charter of King Richard III. bearing date the firft year of his reign. The officers are under oath for the juft performance of their duty: they generally meet in the office on the firft Thurfday in every month, or oftener, if required, where all matters relative to pedigrees and arms of the nobility and gentry, &c. are examined, and if found properly authenticated, are ordered to be entered; but if any difficulty fhould arife, the matter is determined by a majority of voices of the kings, heralds, &c. I mention this to fhew that neither pedigrees or arms can be entered in the Heralds Office, without fufficient proof, and every thing done in due form.

But to refume again the fubject concerning the utility of Parochial Regifters, I would recommend in every entry of a marriage fuch particulars as are fet forth in that for RICHARD MALLETT of Sutton Mallet, in pages 7, 8, and alfo according to the examples in p. 45, 46 aforefaid; and becaufe the married couple, if of feparate parifhes, feldom fettle at the place where they are married, if I may venture to offer my opinion to higher powers, I would recommend moft humbly to their confideration, that every marriage entered in church regifters be to the effect or form following:

MAR-

MARRIAGES, Anno 1690.

ROBERT TRUMAN of Guildford, in com. Surrey, Efq; B. eldeft fon and heir of Charles Truman of Melton-Mowbray, in com. Leic. by Sarah his wife, daughter of Sir John Browne of Browne Park, in com. Northumberland, Knt.

= MARY, only daughter and heir of William Lovely of Strenfham, in com. Worc. S. by Anne his wife, daughter and heir of Stephen Harrington of Harrowbridge, in com. Devon, Efq;

Robert Truman. *Mary Lovely.*

were married, &c.

MARRIAGES, Anno 1700.

JOHN BANISTER of Woodbridge, in com. Suffolk, mercer, B. eldeft fon of John Banifter of Tetbury, in com. Gloc. by Ifabel his wife, daughter of William Pool of Newbury, in com. Berks, malfter,

= MARY, 2d daughter of William Jones of Penfance, in com. Cornwal, merchant, S. by Mary his 2d wife, daughter of Thomas Frampton of Gunby, in com. Linc. grazier,

John Banifter. *Mary Jones.*

were married in this ⎡church⎤ by ⎡banns⎤ with confent of ⎡parents⎤
                    ⎣chapel⎦   ⎣licence⎦   ⎣guardians⎦

this fourteenth day of February One thoufand feven hundred, by me

SOLOMON CHURCHMAN.

In the prefence of
JAMES PRUDOM,
DAVID WATSON.

⎡Rector.⎤
⎢Vicar.⎥
⎣Curate.⎦

According

According to this plan, JOHN BANISTER the hufband, and MARY JONES the wife, not only acknowledge under their hands that the marriage was lawfully folemnized between them, but they alfo record a circumftantial and particular account of their parents: this teftimony is the more to be regarded, becaufe it manifeftly is of great importance to all families to have fuch genealogical accounts tranfmitted to them.

I would further recommend, that in the entries of all BAPTISMS the names of the father and mother of the child, and alfo the name of the mother's father, refidence, degrees, or occupations, be fet forth in like manner as that for EDWARD the fon of Sir John Clopton, in page 15, and the examples in page 46 aforefaid, and then every entry would appear to this purport:

BIRTHS and BAPTISMS.

BANISTER.	JOHN BANISTER, 3d fon of John Banifter of Woodbridge, in com. Suffolk, mercer, and Mary his wife (2d daughter of William Jones of Penfance, in com. Cornwal, merchant) was born the 20th day of October, and baptized the 17th day of the next month following.	1708 Nov. 17.
BANISTER.	JOHN BANISTER, 4th fon of John Banifter of Woodbridge aforefaid, and Mary his wife (2d dau. of William Jones aforefaid) was born the 20th day of November, and baptized the 15th of the next month following.	1709 Dec. 15.

P   The

The same particulars should be observed as much as possible in the entries of BURIALS; and as to those of adults, the addition of husband, wife, widower, widow, and of whom, bachelor, or spinster; and as to men, their rank or employment in life, and from what parish they are buried, might have its use. It would be proper to express whether it be the first, second, third, or fourth child of A. and B. If the person be a parent, it would be also proper to express it thus; that THOMAS A. was buried, who married ANNE B. or, ANNE B. was buried, who married THOMAS A. In short, every method should be practised to identify the person registered: the minister may hereby indeed be subjected to a little more trouble; but as Property and Inheritance will be better secured, and as this is of the last consequence, it is to be presumed the parties will add something to the usual fee.

If Parish Registers were enriched in every entry with these and the like particulars, every register would then exhibit a general history of its several parishioners; pedigrees, titles to arms, to privileges, to estates, would be traced with greater exactness, and a multitude of discoveries made, which, for want of such particulars, are now for the most part rendered egregiously vague and uncertain; supposing, for instance, JOHN BANISTER to have two or more brothers, called also JOHN, who might all marry (such instances we have particularly in the family of WRIGHT of Kilvedon Hall in Essex, as may be seen in the visitation for that county in the Heralds Office, C. 21. p. 10. *) and some of their wives names might be MARY, and their sons called JOHN; or the first-mentioned JOHN might have a second wife, whose name might also be MARY: but now, most likely, there can be but one MARY, daughter of William Jones, whereby the descendents of the said JOHN by that wife will be sufficiently enabled to ascertain their descent from JOHN, and in default of heirs male of William Jones, to claim title also to inheritance, and to arms to be borne quarterly, &c. &c.

That scandalous abuse of all good order, so long connived at, of celebrating Marriages in the Fleet, will always be a reflection upon English liberty, and posterity must sooner or later rue the consequences: for if the Registers of such irregular marriages should chance to be preserved, yet, if produced by

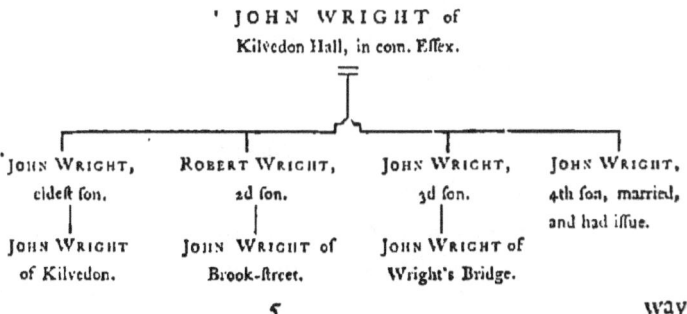

way of evidence in courts of judicature, of what authority can they be for LEGAL proof, when they themselves are ILLEGAL, and especially as those who kept them, being under no manner of check from any superior, might (and probably they often did) make alterations or erasures in their said Registers, or antedate or post-date them as they should be bribed so to do?

The provision made in the late marriage-act, obliging the parties to be married in the parish church where one of them is a parishioner, with the attestation of two witnesses besides the minister, is certainly excellent, since thereby the place and proof of the marriage can in after-times be more readily ascertained; yet is the good purport of this clause scandalously evaded by persons removing from one county or place, and taking lodgings to make themselves parishioners for a month only in another, thereby concealing their true parish and established residence, which of course must render the marriage more obscure and dubious than ever: but as the late marriage-act is now under consideration of higher powers, I shall decline what I intended to say further on this point.

The utility of such minute entries, exemplified aforesaid in Parochial Registers, having been thus far considered, one may reasonably hope that a caution would be altogether needless about the religious conservation of them.

That

That Regifters were from their firft inftitution deemed of very fingular importance to the nation in general, may be collected from the care the Legiflature have from time to time taken about them. The canon of King James I. gives thefe directions, with penalties of a mulct on failure of obfervance: "The regifter fhall be kept in the church in a coffer with three keys, for the minifter and each of the churchwardens; and that on the Sunday the minifter, in the prefence of the churchwardens, fhall make the entries of the week before; to every page (when filled) they fhall all fubfcribe their names: and the churchwardens fhall every year tranfmit a copy thereof to the bifhop's regiftry."

The Parliament alfo have thought the care of Regifters worthy their particular notice; and accordingly by an act of 6º and 7º of King William III. "The minifter neglecting to make the proper entries in the parochial regifter fhall forfeit the fum of One hundred Pounds."

And notwithftanding thefe falutary laws with regard to parochial regifters, it is really amazing to fee, in many places, how very little care is taken about them, while fome of the clergy leave them altogether to the clerk of the parifh, for him to make the entries, who is frequently fo ignorant of his mother-tongue as not to be able to fpell either Chriftian or Surnames; or whofe entries, for want of many neceffary particulars,

ticulars, render the persons thus entered as unknown to the next generation as if they had never existed.

That very Register which I first mentioned for its instructive articles in the entry of its marriages, by being afterwards put under the care of a conceited clerk, who was a stranger to the parish, is become for the time altogether as unintelligible; for here, as well as in other registers, persons are married without specifying their parishes; infants are baptized without the least mention of their parents; and so likewise in the burials; viz.

MARRIAGES.

GEORGE ALLEN and ALICE MOUK.
ELLEN ROWLAND and THOMAS WOODHOUSE.

BAPTISMS.

WILLIAM COCK, crisand.   An infant crisand.

THOMAS TUCKWELL, son of Adam Clark, was born the 20th of June 1722. He stands registered fourteen days before that time; besides Adam Clark was not the father, but the godfather.

JOHN BOSTOCK, son of the Rev. William and Anne of . . . . . . in the county of . . . . . was born in the year 1710. He also stands registered a considerable time before he was born.

BURIALS.

A Child of the Earl of Northumberland
THOMAS RAWLING's wife.   Dr. JOHNSON's lady.
DOROTHY GIFFARD's daughter.   Old Father BEADLE.
A prentice of Mr. SLIFORD.   Old Father ERITAGE.
a nurse child, a Londoner's child, a Londoner   Good
, 3 after.

Good wife GOODALL.   Old good wife LEWES.
Old Mother PUMMELL.   BLACK JOHN.
Mother STUDDY.   Farmer BROWNE.
Gammer SMITH.   Tipling TOMLINSON.
The widow MICHELL, from the Ames H. (alms-houfe).
An oul man from the W. H. (work-houfe).

Certainly many of the above are no other than nick-names. What different ufage I have frequently found in one and the fame regifter! and I choofe to inftance particularly herein as a caution, with fubmiffion, to all minifters officiating, to make the entries of marriages, baptifms, and burials themfelves, and never truft fo facred a depofitum, as is too often the cafe, to the blunders of an illiterate clerk, which is thus, and in many other inftances, fubjected to abufe.

A gentleman having prepared himfelf to embark for the Eaft Indies, and being of age, proceeded to fettle an affair which could not be done before; and as the nature of it was fuch, that a proof of his age was required by a certificate from the parifh regifter, he had recourfe thereto, and found that he ftood regiftered about two years after the time that he was baptized; which unlucky circumftance prevented his going abroad, and proved a great difappointment to him.

Another gentleman died, and left a confiderable fum of money in the funds; the relations of the deceafed claimed as

next

next of kin; but as it was neceffary to prove his death and burial prior to the recovery, had recourfe to the parifh regifter, where indeed they found the Surname was entered, but the Chriftian name was that of a WOMAN, inftead of a MAN, which, though no more than a miftake, occafioned fome trouble and expence to the parties concerned.

A natural daughter, born in a certain parifh, had 5000l. left her, to be paid when fhe was of age; previous to receiving her legacy a certificate of her age or baptifm from the church regifter was required; to which fhe had recourfe, but in vain; for, after the ftricteft examination, no entry of her name could be found, notwithftanding fhe was well afiured fhe was baptized in the church, which, luckily for her, was proved by feveral living witneffes. The like omiffion by accident might have happened in any other parifh; but as this particular circumftance opened a difcovery of many more omiffions in the fame regifter, I have thought proper to mention it, as the difficulties refulting from fuch miftakes are numberlefs.

I had once occafion to confult the regifter of . . . . in the county of . . . . . . when I was directed to the cottage of a poor labouring man, as clerk of the parifh; he not being at home, I informed the children of what I wanted; upon which they pulled out the drawer of an old table, where, among much rubbifh of rufty iron, &c. I found the regifter greatly injured, by the handling, perhaps, of his children, &c. and had any one an intereſt therein, might have either altered or carried it off without diſcovery.

This puts me in mind of another yet more flagrant inſtance of abuſe concerning the regiſter of the pariſh of ...... in the county of ...... that the clerk being a taylor, and keeper of the regiſters (according to common report in the pariſh) ſo often as he wanted ſlips of parchment for meaſures, made no ſcruple to cut out of the old written regiſter ſixteen leaves, and ſomething more, for that purpoſe. The regiſter was a large folio, and appears formerly to have conſiſted of eighteen leaves; there lately remained but one whole leaf and two bits, containing entries from the year 1633 to 1639, and ſome odd dates from that time to 1645.

But now of ſuch eſſential notices, if once loſt, how are they ever to be recovered? you will ſay, from the regiſter of the biſhop of the dioceſe, whither extracts from every pariſh regiſter are, or ſhould be, annually ſent to be ſafely depoſited. But what if here alſo ſhould be found neglect? and ſuch as muſt neceſſarily tend to the ſetting aſide the above canon (and virtually alſo the act of parliament) in not properly ſecuring ſuch extracts from the injuries of time, or other accidents.

Of the above inſtances of neglect I was ſome time ſince an eye-witneſs in the cathedral church of . . . . . . Under a ſtair-caſe in a place on the north ſide of the north iſle, upon the damp ground without the ſecurity of a door, free for any one to go to, I found a promiſcuous heap of extracts of regiſters, ſome very fairly tranſcribed, from the different pariſhes of the dioceſs: theſe, by reaſon of the damps, were expoſed to depredations equally as deſtructive as thoſe ſaid to be committed by the taylor; and probably are, if not ſince removed to ſome ſecurer place, either loſt or become illegible.

But the neceſſity of a religious conſervation of theſe extracts ariſes not merely by way of evidence, in caſe the original ſhould be loſt, but alſo in caſe of forgery in thoſe originals, either by interpolations or eraſures, or the like; for as theſe extracts are to be made annually, and ſent to the ſaid regiſtry, any appeal to them, when properly preſerved, will be the ready means for detection of ſuch forgery, by giving the entry exactly as it ſtood in the original.

And ſuch an appeal I remember was once made to the regiſtry of the biſhop of Sarum, upon ſuſpicion that a certain pariſh regiſter in that dioceſe had been falſified; but how or in what manner was not to be diſcovered from the regiſter itſelf; when upon examination of the extract thus appealed to, and readily produced, the whole fraud was laid open; for by

comparing

comparing the copy with the original it plainly appeared that the true name, regularly entered in its proper place, had been quite altered to another by an erafure of two letters in the middle, and inferting upon that erafure three other different letters in their room; and then by entering the firft name under a date of more than two years later, in order to prevent fuperannuation for a fcholarfhip in one of our univerfities: but the detection of the fraud proved the lofs of the fcholarfhip, and the immediate junior fucceeded, who otherwife in courfe muft have been fuperannuated. But I muft obferve, however, that during this forgery the regifter was in the clerk's cuftody: but quære, in cafe of forgeries fubfequent to this, who will be moft to blame, the clerk, or his principal?

Let us here again obferve that the value of regifters, and confequently of fuch extracts from them, is of late very greatly enhanced by the difcontinuance of vifitations in the feveral counties of England by the officers of arms; for in fuch vifitations the nobility and gentry did enter their feveral lineal and collateral defcents, and thereby did connect themfelves with their firft recorded anceftor: from this care and prudence of our anceftors a good extraction is tranfmitted to their pofterity. That this is a real fortune abroad, every one knows who has travelled into Germany or France; and alfo that no perfon in thofe countries, however rich, can enjoy any honourable poft or employment unlefs he can fhew proof of a good defcent;

scent; qualifications for scholarships, &c. at home; commandries, and orders ecclesiastical, civil, and military abroad, &c.

But although such entries are still regularly made in the Heralds Office by many cautious persons, for the sake of their posterity (the expence attending such entries being very inconsiderable) yet because it is not done so generally as it ought, recourse must now frequently be had for descents, for legitimacy, for privileges, &c. to these parochial registers and the extracts from them.

It was but lately at the assize at Newcastle upon Tyne, that Mr. Gillam, near Rumford in Essex, proved himself the rightful heir to an estate in Northumberland to the value of about 40 or 50,000 l. The estates in suspense, or which were lately so for want of heirs, of the family of STOTE of Jesmond in Northumberland; also that of BARNESLEY of Barnesley Hall in Worcestershire, and several others, are recent instances of the value of Registers, and of the utility that may arise to the community from them when correct, and carefully preserved.

This utility is pressed the stronger on my mind from the labour and difficulty my worthy acquaintance Mr. STEVENS TOTTON underwent for some years in a cause * finally concluded in Michaelmas Term last; wherein he had the pedigree of a

* Jesson and Wither versus Brewer.

family

family of some consequence to prove; and though he was not under a necessity of going further back for a common ancestor than the year 1590, yet by means of erasures in some regisers, and bad writing in others; some being torn in pieces and appropriated to various uses; others kept in damp places and suffered to moulder away, &c. his difficulties were amazing, and must have been unsurmountable, had he not exercised an uncommon degree of patience and perseverance. He had recourse to almost every record office in the kingdom, and was obliged to be at a very great expence, chiefly owing to defects in the registers; which expence would have been saved, if the parochial registers had been properly kept.

When at any time a minister is desired to consult the register for a parochial name, and that name occurs not, the minister should certify in some such form as this; *I have consulted the Register, and cannot find, in or about the time mentioned, the name required.* The reason of this caution arises from a recent fact; the minister of a certain parish was desired to consult his register for a certain name about a given time; he answered by letter under his own hand, that no such name could be found: he was desired a second time to consult his register, the same answer was returned. Some time after a person accidentally looked into the register, and found what was required. The truth was, the minister had never examined the register, but had left it to the care of his clerk, who was more than half blind.

S   As

As a mark of esteem particularly due to the care of another minister, upon an application like the preceding, I shall take the liberty to give an extract from his own letter:

After giving an account of the searches he had made in his register, and lamenting the loss of ancient monuments, which he imagined were all destroyed when the old church was pulled down in order to be rebuilt; "I searched (says he) "through a period of fifty years, before I could find any thing "at all to the purpose, through pages so wretchedly written, "that they put me in mind of the obscure hand in Queen's "college library, Oxford, which neither native nor foreigner "hath ever yet been able to read: this task cost me two "days hard study in spelling out the dates and names as I "went along, which I hope are discoveries answerable to your "wishes and expectations; but if there be any mistakes, blame "not me, but my predecessors, for the above are true copies "to the best of my knowledge." That respect which is due to this gentleman's attention, would not permit me to pass it over in silence.

Before I conclude this discourse on Registers, I cannot help taking notice of and commending the good old custom which still prevails in many parts of England, of entering marriages, births, and burials in family Bibles, Prayer-books, &c. but as entries made therein are seldom so fully expressed as they should be, be, I will beg leave to recommend the curious reader to see that memorial which Mr. Guthrie has introduced in his English Peerage, p. 304, from one drawn up by Sir William Cavendish for himself, his three wives, and sixteen children; and after Sir William's death signed by the Lady Elizabeth Hardwick his widow, as one of the most remarkable examples of its kind, and as a better can hardly be given.

To this collection of examples concerning Registers the matriculation books in the university of Oxford claim particular notice: having occasion some time ago to examine the date of a young gentleman's entry in that university, I was surprized and pleased to find the great exactness with which such entries are made; for not only the day and year of the entry, but also the age of the young gentleman, and the Christian name and residence of the father were specified, and also whether he was the elder or younger son. I make no doubt but the same exactness is observed in the university of Cambridge.

And that I may not pass over any thing that has the least tendency to preserve the memory of families, I shall introduce a few sepulchral Inscriptions, taken during my residence in Flanders, Holland, &c. to shew how usual it is, even among the common people of those parts, to give the Surnames of their wives on tomb-stones, to which very few in England attend.

MAES-

MAESTRICHT.

In the church of our LADY.

M. S.

Viduæ, Clientes, Pauperes, Cives, Forum,
Aſtræa, Sophia, Hiſtoria, Muſarum chori
Nequiere morti eripere Galenum ſuum.
Sic nempe cautum eſt, omnibus reſtat mori,
Sed vita juſtis redditur, malis perit.

JACOBO GALENO ſibiq; ANGELA GREEFTIA, ut pridem tori, ſic tandē tumuli conſors R. C. Obiere ille an. Chriſtiano CIƆIƆCXXII. xii kal. Feb. Hæc CIƆIƆC...

ANTWERP.

In the church of our LADY.

CHRISTOPHORO PLANTINO,
Turonenſi civi & incolæ Antverpiano
Architypographo Regio,
Pietate, Prudentia, acrimonia ingenii magna,
Conſtantia & Labore maximo,
cujus induſtriâ atque operâ
infinita opera, vetera, nova,
magno & hujus, & futuri ſeculi bono
in lucem prodierunt.

JOAN RIVIERA conjux & lib. hæredeſque,
illa optimo viro, hi parenti
mœſti poſuerunt.
Tu qui tranſis & hæc legis, bonis manibus
bene precare.
Vixit annos LXXV. deſiit hic vivere
kalend. quinctilibus aº Chriſti CIƆ· IƆ. XXCIX.

D. O. M.
LEONARDUS VERMOELEN, Eleemosinarius
& MARIA VAN ROOSENDAEL conjux.
Obiit ille 20. Junuarii 1703.
Illa vero 1. Decembris 1708.

In the church of St. Michael.

PHILIPPO RUBENIO I. C.
Johannis Civis & Senatoris Antverpiæ Fil.
magni Lipsii discipulo & alumno,
cujus Doctrinam poenè assecutus
Modestiam feliciter adæquavit
Bruxellæ præsidi Richardoto
Romæ Ascanio Cardinali Columnæ
ab Epistolis & Studiis
S. P. Q. Antverpiensi à secretis
Abiit, non obiit, virtute, & scriptis sibi superstes
V kal. Septemb. anno Christi CIƆ DC XL. Æ. XXXIIX.
Marito bene merenti MARIA DE MOY.
Duûm ex illo Liberorum CLARÆ & PHILIPPI mater
Propter illius ejusque matris MARIÆ PYFELINCX
Sepulchrum, hoc mœroris, & amoris sui
Monumentum P. C.
PHILIPPUS RUBENIUS PHILIPPI F. J. C.
Huic urbi à secretis, & senator decessit
V Octobris 1678. ætatis 67.

D. O. M. S.
MARIÆ PIPELINGIÆ prudentiss. lectiss. fœminæ, quæ matrimonio
juncta fuit JOANNI RUBENIO J. C. & senatori Antverpiensi, eoque or-
bata viduitatem ad diem fati per annos XXII. religiose coluit, PHILIPPUS &
PETRUS

Petrus Paulus Rubenii cum nepotibus è filia Blandina, piæ matri &
B. M. F. Vixit annos LXX. M. VI. D. XXIX. obiit XIV. kal. Novemb.
CIƆ· IƆC. VIII.

In the church of St. James.

ALBERTUS RUBENIUS Petri Pauli Fil..
Regi. Cathol. in fanctiore confilio
à fecretis hic fitus eft.
Qui Politioris omnis Litteraturæ,
Hiftoriæ, Greciæ et Romanæ, reique
Antiquariæ cognitione nemini cedens,
Honoris medio in curfu deceffit
An. Sal. M. DC. LVII. kal. Oct. æta. XLIII.
. D. Clara del Monte
Mariti chariffimi defiderio ægra
vixque elapfo menfe ipfum fecuta,
facro perpetuò in hoc facello pie
fundata obiit XXV Novemb. M. DC. LVII..
Ætat. XXXIX.

D. O. M.
DANIELIS FORMENT & CLARÆ STAPPAERT conjugum,
obiit hæc 20 Januarij 1639. Ille vero 3 Junii 1643.

Hier leet begraeven Jouffrouw ANNA LOMMELINO, weduwe Wylen
Bartholomeus Geribaldi, doghter van Bernardo Lommelino, Genevois, fterft 1612, 10 Januarij.

Resurrectioni Sacrum
PETRUS ROBYNS & BARBARA de WINDELE,
conjuges, quos fingularis amor & concordia conjunxit, hoc condi tumulo voluere.
O beatam mutui amoris conftantiam! CIƆ IƆ CXIII.

NAMUR.

NAMUR.
In the church of St. John.

Icy gift Madame ANNE CATH. d'BRUMAIGNE efpoufe d'WALTER PHILIPPE d'COLYEAR, Genl d'Infanterie, Colonel d'un Regiment de Infanterie Ecoffoife au fervice de leurs Hautes Puiffances les Etats Generaux des Provinces Unies, Governeur de leur part de la ville et du chateau du Namur, laquelle trefpaffa le 10 Septembre, l'an 1738.

AMSTERDAM.

Hier leyt begraven het lighaam van Juffrouwe MARIA WEMELL, Huyfvrouwe van de Heir JAN VANACRE, brouwer tot Haarlem, en dogter van de Heir JACOBUS WEMELL, koopman tot Dort, by zyn Huyfvrouwe MARIA BIRNE, dogter van de Heir ROBERT BIRNE tot Corke in Ireland. Geftorven op den 25 May 1690, oud 28 Jaaren.

To thefe foreign infcriptions I will fubjoin a few which I tranfcribed at

EDINBURGH.
In the Gray Fryers church-yard.

Memoriæ chariffimæ fuæ conjugis CATHERINÆ TOD quæ deceffit 27 Januarij 1679, monumentum hoc extrui curavit maritus fuperftes WALTERUS CHEISLIE de Dalry mercator et civis Edinburgenfis.

Memoriæ chariffimæ conjugis ELIZABETHÆ PATON JOANNES CUNNINGHAM ad Enterkin facræ regiæ majeftati & ad ipfius fignetum fcriba monumentum hoc extruendum curavit.

Hic jacet ANNA RAYE uxor JOHANNIS CARSTAIRS, fœmina lectiffima, quæ conjugi chariffima vixit, & magno omnium bonorum luctu & defiderio morte immatura prærepta eft anno Dom. 1632, menfis Julij 14, Ætatis vero 29.

[72]

Hic jacent exuviæ ALEXANDRI BETHUNE de Longhirdmondſton, ſigneto regio ſcribæ; ex priſca & præclara familia de Balfour ortum habentis. Vir erat prudentiâ, pietate & induſtria haud leviter imbutus. Ex uxore ſua MARJORANA KENNEDIE, cum qua triginta annos conjunctiſſime vixit numeroſam ſobolem ſuſcepit. Ob. 9. Novembris 1672, Æt. ſuæ 57.

In HOLY ROOD HOUSE church-yard.

Memoriæ dilectiſſimi conjugis JOANNIS PATERSONI, qui cum ſuaviſſimo matrimonii vinculo 35 plus minus annos tranſegiſſet; & aliquoties Balivi munere in vico Canongate functus eſſet; obiit anno Chriſti 1663, April 23. Ætatis 63. Amoris & officij ergo, monumentum hoc dicavit AGNETA LYELL.

LEITH, &c.

Here lyeth MARION MAC KYNE, ſpouſe to JOHN WATSON, &c.

Here reſts the corps of MICHAEL BAKER, &c. &c. and ELIZABETH WRIGHT his ſpouſe, who departed this life, &c.

Here lyes THOMAS HALL, &c. and JANE HORN his wife, &c.

Here lyes MARGARET BOTHWICK, ſpouſe to THOMAS ZEMAN, &c.

To the memory of BETHIA MURRAY, ſpouſe to HUGH MOSMAN, &c.

By theſe examples we ſee how exact and particular people abroad are, as well as in Scotland, to maintain the true courſe of inheritance, by inſcribng on monuments or grave-ſtones the SURNAMES of their wives; for the like reaſons we ſhould never omit to perpetuate the ſame here, as thereby inſcriptions would certainly be more uſeful to poſterity; for the monuments of the dead would then maintain the pedigrees of the living.

Upon

Upon this occasion I cannot help taking notice of a great impropriety which generally prevails in England. How often do we see inscriptions in these forms?

> Here lieth the body of MARGARET, wife of THOMAS LONDON, who died, &c. &c.

> Here lieth the body of MARGARET LONDON, wife of THOMAS LONDON, who died, &c.

No information is hereby conveyed as to the wife's family; and the repetition of the Surname is idle, if her maiden name is to be suppressed: as it is necessary to ascertain as much as possible what family is connected, for instance, with that of THOMAS LONDON, that may be done with no more expence and trouble, after the example of the foreign inscriptions, or those in Scotland:

> Here lieth the body of MARGARET HACKNEY, wife of THOMAS LONDON, who died 10 Aug. 1700.

But as it is of importance to be more particular, I would recommend the methods following:

> Here lieth the body of MARGARET, late wife of THOMAS LONDON of this parish, brewer, and daughter of THOMAS HACKNEY of Yarmouth, in the county of Norfolk, master and mariner. She died 10 Aug. 1700, aged 34 years, and left issue one son THOMAS, and one daughter MARGARET.

> Here lie the bodies of ROBERT TRUMAN, late of Guildford, in the county of Surrey, Esq; and of ANNE his wife, only daughter and heir of WILLIAM LOVELY of Strenfham, in the county of Worcester, Esq;

He died the 15th day of Auguft 1705, aged 45 years.
She died the 20th day of November 1706, aged 50 years, and left iffue three fons and three daughters; viz.
ROBERT, JOHN, WILLIAM, SARAH, ANNE, and MARY.

One thing more I muft mention before I quit this fubject, and that is, I could wifh that no initial letters were permitted on grave-ftones, as T. L. died: the names ought to be at full length, as THOMAS LONDON, &c. and if the circumftances of the perfon permit, as nearly fimilar to the entry in the Regifter as poffible.

To thefe remarks I fhall add, as tending fo much to the prefent difcourfe, what that eminent lawyer Sir HENRY CHAUNCY, Knt. obferves in the preface to his Antiquities of Hertfordfhire, wherein, fpeaking of his family pedigree introduced in that work, and that he could not obtain fuch helps as he could have wifhed, to fet forth the genealogies of other gentlemen in like manner as his own, " I would (fays he) have given fuller
" accounts of them, there being now greater ufe of thefe than
" formerly, to make out claims by defcent upon expiration
" of any long terms or eftates, fuch cafes often happening,
" which are difficult to be proved, when Inquifitions POST
" MORTEM are determined by act of parliament, the brafs
" plates taken away from grave-ftones, and regifters of chrift-
" nings, marriages, and burials are loft, or rendered fo im-
" perfect, that many times the names and furnames of chil-
" dren

" dren baptized, or the perfons married or buried, with the
" places of their refidence, their titles or additions, cannot be
" difcovered; and there are no other evidences but deeds, that
" fometimes mention not two generations, feldom more, which
" may occafion great inconveniences hereafter, except fome
" prudent methods are taken to prevent them, by conftant
" regular entries of defcents in the COLLEGE of ARMS, their
" proper REPOSITORY."

To defcant on the vaft importance of thefe meafures would feem needlefs, as there are fo many confiderable eftates in the kingdom at this time wanting heirs, from a neglect of arms and pedigrees being duly regulated, and entered in the HERALDS OFFICE; and were it not for the frequent proofs of affinity and confanguinity obtained from the faid Office, fuch inftances would be very numerous.

The laft vifitations for the feveral counties of England were made between the years 1660 and 1688; fuch of the nobility and gentry as have not brought down the continuations of their pedigrees, by having recourfe to deeds, marriage fettlements, wills, parifh regifters, fepulchral infcriptions, &c. may eafily join themfelves to their old family ftock; but if not done in this generation, the next may be too late, and the memory of families and their connexions by neglect may become irrecoverably loft.

The substance and intent of what hath been hitherto observed may be reduced to the following particulars: it is of importance to every family, not excepting the meanest, to pay some regard to their pedigrees, and consequently every circumstance, whether of a public or private nature, which tends to preserve or elucidate Genealogical History, should be attended to with the most religious care.

I. PAROCHIAL REGISTERS.

Concerning which, but with great submission to superior judges, I would propose, that all old Registers that require it be repaired, and that for every register large wide folio books well bound be provided with good vellum leaves (parchment is improper; unless pounced as customary it will scarce admit the ink, and if pounced, it will subject the parchment and writing to decay); that the leaves be numbered, and an inch margin be left at the top, bottom, and on each side of every folio or page; that all entries be within the margin to prevent the writing being defaced by turning over the book with a wet finger or thumb; and for dispatch and the conveniency of the minister, as well as those who shall have occasion to consult the register, there be a general index at the end of each book with references to the names in the several pages, which will be very useful and save much trouble in searching, especially in large parishes: that registers should not always be kept in the veſtry (or cheſt in the pariſh church) unleſs very dry, or a fire be now-and-then made, but rather that they be kept in ſome ſecure, dry place in the parſonage-houſe, guarded however from fire or other accidents. The miniſter muſt on all accounts have a key occaſionally to conſult them. The entries of marriages, baptiſms, and burials ſhould be always made by the gentleman officiating himſelf; but in caſe he ſhould become incapable by the infirmities of old age, or otherwiſe, and cannot write a fair hand himſelf, a proper perſon ſhould be engaged to make the entries in a ſtrong legible hand, under the inſpection of the ſaid miniſter or churchwardens: the miniſter ſhould alſo be under obligation never to permit the pariſh regiſter to be lent to any one whomſoever, unleſs required by a public court of juſtice; nor ſuffer any eraſures or alterations whatever. If through inadvertency the entry of a baptiſm ſhould be made among the burials, or vice verſâ, that it be not eraſed with a knife, but that a line be drawn through the entry with black ink, and a note made in the margin of the miſtake, and reference to the folio where the entry is or ſhould have been made.—Many of theſe remarks will, I preſume, appear reaſonable at firſt view; and the avoiding Raſures in regiſters would very often prevent frauds, and even the ſuſpicion of fraud, when occaſionally laid before courts of juſtice, and make it hereafter abundantly eaſier to prove a pedigree from pariſh regiſters, to the ſatisfaction of a judge or jury, than it is at preſent.

II. INSCRIPTIONS,

Either on ERECT MONUMENTS, or TOMB-STONES, in Churches or Church-yards.

Concerning Funeral Honours; " Epitaphs (fays Camden) have been always moſt refpective, for in them love was ſhewn to the deceaſed, and their memory was continued to poſterity; friends were comforted, and the reader put in mind of human frailty." And Sir Henry Chauncy, ſpeaking of preſerving the inſcriptions on monuments and grave-ſtones, ſays, " Theſe being memorials of our once-flouriſhing anceſtors, deſigned to perpetuate their remembrance to future ages, are of no deſpicable uſe to Heralds in tracing pedigrees, or Lawyers in making out titles to eſtates."

If a church is to be repaired or rebuilt, great care ſhould be obſerved to take copies of every monumental inſcription or coat of arms; the ſame care ſhould alſo extend to church windows, which often contain painted arms, written labels, &c. Mr. WEEVER, in his preface concerning Funeral Monuments, obſerves that in other kingdoms the monuments of the dead are preſerved, and their inſcriptions or epitaphs are regiſtered in the church books: he juſtly laments the barbarous and inhuman practice (to the ſhame of his time) of monuments " broken down and almoſt ruinated, their brazen inſcriptions erafed, torne away, and pilfered; by which deformidable act the honourable memory of many vertuous and noble perſons deceaſed is extinguiſhed, and the true underſtanding of divers families in theſe realmes (who have deſcended of thoſe worthy perſons aforeſaid) is ſo darkened, as the true courſe of their inheritance is thereby partly interrupted." Grieving (as he obſerves) at this inſufferable injury, offered as well to the living as the dead, out of reſpect he bore to venerable antiquity, and the due regard to continue the remembrance of the deceaſed to future ages, it was that he collected ſuch memorials of the deceaſed as were then remaining undefaced.

To theſe obſervations, which I thought proper to premiſe, I ſhall now reſume my own: Many grave-ſtones are often half, and others wholly covered with pews, &c. many alſo are broken, and by the ſinking of graves not only inſcriptions are loſt, but the beauty of the church defaced; all theſe and many other evils might be remedied, in caſe every pariſh was obliged to have, in like manner as abroad, a monumental book, to be kept with the regiſter, wherein every inſcription ſhould be fairly written, under the inſpection of the miniſter officiating; for which purpoſe a fee ſhould be paid: nor would it be amiſs, if every pariſh had the ichnography of the church on a large ſcale, with proper references to each perſon's grave or family vault. This ought eſpecially to be done when any old church is repaired, or pulled down in order to be rebuilt.

The

[80]

The late Earl of WESTMORLAND, when he rebuilt his church at Meerworth in Kent, from the veneration he had to antiquity and the memory of his noble anceſtors, as well as thoſe of the pariſhioners in general, took all the care imaginable to reinſtate the ſeveral monuments and grave-ſtones, with their inſcriptions; even the very meaneſt head-ſtone in the church-yard was replaced in due form. The curious painted glaſs of the old church windows (which repreſented the arms, quarterings, and ſupporters of his lordſhip's family, as well as many others of the nobility) was carefully taken down and preſerved, and afterwards with the greateſt exactneſs put up in the new church, which is not only very ornamental, but may hereafter be uſeful to poſterity.

In like manner JAMES CLITHEROE of Boſton Houſe, in the county of Middleſex, Eſq; before the old church of Brentford was pulled down, to preſerve as much as poſſible every memorial of antiquity that remained undefaced in that church, has had the ichnography thereof very curiouſly taken, with references to every grave and monument, and exact copies of the inſcriptions, that thereby the ſame ſhall be duly replaced when the church is rebuilt.

By theſe notable inſtances of public ſpirit to preſerve the monuments of the dead, it is to be hoped that the living, by their good example, will (when occaſion ſhall require) take the ſame care as to every other church of the kingdom.

III.

III. IMPRESSIONS of SEALS to Deeds, Wills, &c.

Have been found in genealogical matters to be of signal service. Our books have carefully preserved such wherever they could be procured. Deeds began to be dated in the reign of King Edward I. though not constantly so, says Lord COKE in his Institutes, before the reign of King Edward II.

The use of Seals is very ancient: Sir WILLIAM DUGDALE, in his Antiquities of Warwickshire, observes that King Edward the Confessor, upon his foundation of Westminster Abbey, was the first in England who put his seal to his charter, according to the custom of the Normans, with whom he had been educated. The king only, and some of the nobility, at first used seals, chiefly with their images on horseback thereon, afterwards, as arms became settled and hereditary, the gentlemen of the better sort used them on their seals; and about King Edward IIId's time seals became common. Before the subscribing names to ancient charters and evidences they were only signed with seals, probably because in those early days very few people could write, and which, as NISBET observes, contributed greatly to the regularity of arms: he tells us it was enacted by several statutes, that every freeholder should have his proper seal of arms, and should either compeer himself at the head court of the shire, or send his attorney with the said seal; and those who wanted such seals were to be amerciat or fined. Every gentleman used then to send his seal to the clerk of the court in lead, in order to compare with other sealings, for fear of counterfeits; for it was reckoned, says NISBET, no less crime than forgery to counterfeit another man's seal, for which severe punishments were inflicted; and so particularly careful were people of their seals in those days, that in case one was lost, no means were wanting by public proclamation to have it restored, lest any one might use it to the prejudice of another. MACKENZIE observes, that of old the appending of a seal was sufficient in charters without the subscription of the party, and that the custom of sealing without subscription continued in Scotland till the year 1540, when King James V. by an act did ordain that all evidences should be subscribed as well as sealed, &c.

As impressions of seals have been found in genealogical matters to be very useful, as I observed before, I cannot therefore help lamenting the present prevailing custom, I mean the sealing a will, &c. not with the seal of the testator, but of the person who drew it up; and also of affixing the same seal three or four times to a deed, when several parties are concerned: surely the most rational way seems to be, that each person who signs his own name, should also affix his own seal.

IV.

IV. WILLS and ADMINISTRATIONS.

That Wills in general (the solemn instruments whereby people manifest their minds as to the disposal of their estates, goods, &c.) are some of the best proofs of consanguinity, will, I apprehend, be readily acknowledged; but these, for want of some particulars, such as the surname of the wife, her father and mother's residence, &c. are not so useful as they might be; I would therefore, that the maternal ancestors of families may hereafter be better known, recommend to every person who makes a will to express himself in the following form:

I WILLIAM SMITH of Honiton, in the county of Devon, clothier, third son of TIMOTHY SMITH, late of the parish of St. Dunstan in the West, London, woollen-draper, deceased, by MARY his wife, daughter of JOHN BROWNE of Cramlington in Northumberland, do make, &c. I leave to ANNE my now wife, daughter of JOHN SAUNDERS of Honiton aforesaid: Item, to my eldest son WILLIAM (by my first wife SARAH, daughter of SAMPSON GREENLAND of Ottery St. Mary, in the said county of Devon): Item, to SARAH my only daughter (by my present wife) wife of SAMUEL HAYMAN of Sidbury, in the said county of Devon, Gent. Item, to my daughter-in-law MARTHA, only daughter of BENJAMIN HEARD of Sidmouth, Gent. and wife to my said son WILLIAM, &c.

As Wills are admitted as evidence in the courts of law, every thing which tends to make them more useful, or to preserve them and procure ready access to them, is of consequence. How many obscure courts are there at present, in which

which wills are depofited, which are probably unknown even to perfons moft concerned in them! I hope I fhall not be thought too prefuming, if I take the liberty to offer a fcheme which may remedy this evil: The original wills might be preferved in the manner they now are; but I would propofe a GENERAL OFFICE in London, in which fhould be depofited attefted copies of every will and adminiftration throughout the kingdom; what are now difperfed both in the greater and leffer courts, would thereby be collected in one place, and accefs to confult any particular will would be rendered much eafier: at prefent, indeed, every will depofited in the PREROGATIVE COURT is fairly copied in books for that purpofe; but I apprehend this is not done in the provincial courts, and confequently a will deftroyed by time, duft, vermin, or other accidents, becomes an irreparable lofs.

For a long while the wills, &c. in St. Paul's church lay undigefted and neglected; the excellent order to which they will foon be reduced, is owing to the direction of that publicfpirited prelate the Right Rev. Dr. RICHARD OSBALDESTON, the prefent Lord Bifhop of London.

There is another article of the greateft confequence to every civil community, and to this kingdom in particular; I mean, to eftablifh in LONDON,

V.

V. A General Register of MARRIAGES throughout the Kingdom, with Indexes, Containing the Surnames of both Man and Woman.

Such a regifter might eafily be compiled, if every officiating minifter was directed to tranfmit to this Office, twice at leaft every year, a lift of the marriages in his refpective parifh, written, it were to be wifhed, with his own hand, and figned by him; if not, at leaft to be certified by him, and witneffed by the churchwardens. The clergy, to whom undoubtedly a proper fee is due for confulting the regifter of their refpective parifhes, may be indemnified by adding fomething to the prefent fee for regiftering the marriage, referving ftill a right to their fee in cafe it fhould be found advifeable to confult the original regifter. And here

I cannot omit declaring how fenfible I am of the obliging regard which the clergy in general have always paid to any application I, or any of my brethren, have been obliged to make to them in the courfe of our office; ever ready to confult their regifters, and fpeedy and exact in their extracts: and left any one fhould think himfelf injured by any thing which has been faid in this pamphlet, I hope it will be confidered as faid from no kind of difrefpect, but from a zeal to the public fervice, and by way of caution for the future.

As a general tranquillity is now happily re-eſtabliſhed, it is to be wiſhed that all perſons intruſted with the chief management of public offices would take under their conſideration the preſent ſtate of them; and that all manuſcripts which in anywiſe relate or pertain to particular offices ſhould be given or reſtored to their proper Repoſitories.

The uſes and advantages of general offices in the Metropolis for collecting into one body (properly digeſted and indexed) papers, &c. which now lie unknown and ſcattered in various parts of the kingdom, are too obvious to be further inſiſted upon: the nation will, I hope, ſoon be ſenſible of this fact, when the AUGMENTATION OFFICE is completed; a work of the higheſt conſequence and utility, in which Gentlemen of the moſt diſtinguiſhed abilities are now conſtantly employed.

The Records alſo in the ROLLS Chapel and the TOWER are now, through the indefatigable care of the ingenious Mr. ROOKE, digeſted in the moſt methodical manner, and thereby rendered more than ever of public utility.

VI. CASTLES, PALACES, PRIVATE HOUSES, &c.

Often contain on the walls or windows the moſt ancient marks of family honours, ſuch as arms, creſts, ſupporters, mottos, badges, &c. As theſe are more immediately the concern

cern of each family, I can only take the liberty to propose the following method to guard against the injuries of time before it be too late, to have attested copies or draughts made of them, which might be preserved in the family, or deposited in the HERALDS OFFICE.

That eminent lawyer WILLIAM BURTON, Esq; in the preface to his Description of Leicestershire, speaking of arms, &c. affirms, " That the antiquity of a church window, for the " proof of a match and issue, hath been delivered in evi- " dence to a jury at an assize, and been accepted;" and so sensible was he that these ancient memorials might be still more useful to posterity, he collected them and the inscriptions of the tombs; because, as he observes, " they may rectify armories and genealogies, and give such testimony and proof as may put an end to many differences."

In confirmation of events similar to the above, I know three families who have acquired estates by virtue of preserving the arms and escutcheons of their ancestors; and of damages lately recovered by a certain parish against a person for the removal of a wall of three hundred years standing, owing to a coat of arms being carved upon one of the stones saved from the ruins, and brought to me to examine; which arms, though much defaced by time, I soon discovered to pertain to a certain alderman of London; in consequence of which his will

was

was found, and the matter therein fully explained. Other inftances I could give, but thefe I think will be fufficient to fhew, that however the ignorant or inconfiderate clafs of the people may contemn or defpife a coat of arms, yet it ferves many important purpofes, and never can lofe that veneration which is inviolably due to it from the noble and illuftrious.

To fee arms or enfigns of honour on feals, plate, coaches, or fet forth in churches, public halls, maps, dedications to books, &c. which are univerfally known to be the right of particular families, ufurped, or licentioufly taken by perfons who never were legally invefted with fuch enfigns, feems repugnant to reafon as well as the ancient and prefent laws of arms, and indeed to the fenfe of the wifeft nations; and if fome care is not taken to check thefe abufes, great inconveniences muft hereafter enfue to pofterity. And here I cannot help taking notice of people who now bear arms to which they have no manner of right, and which are no where to be found in the HERALDS OFFICE. The ufual plea is, that their grants, &c. were deftroyed, with other books and papers in the Heralds Office, by the great fire of London anno 1666; I therefore think it proper to acquaint the Public that no one book or paper was loft in the great fire; every record was removed to a room in the palace of WHITEHALL, afterwards to another room in the palace of WESTMINSTER, formerly called the Queen's Court, and public notice was given that the HERALDS OFFICE was

kept

kept there: only one book was loft in the removal, a vifitation of Kent; but this lofs is in a great meafure fupplied by other vifitations of Kent ftill preferved; one of which was taken but two years before; and alfo by feveral copies of vifitations of Kent collected by the ingenious JOHN PHILIPOT, Efq; Somerfet Herald, original compiler of the Antiquities of Kent.

Almoft all nations have maintained that no perfon can affume arms without lawful authority; and whoever prefumes to bear them without the king's licence, or having firft obtained the Earl Marfhal's warrant to the proper officers eftablifhed by patent under the great feal of Great Britain to grant the fame, infringes upon the fovereign, the fountain from whom all honours fhould fpring. The king's children do not bear arms without a licence from the fovereign their royal father directed to the Earl Marfhal, &c. neither can a perfon, though dignified with the title of Baronet, Knight, or Efquire, when created by the royal favour a peer of this realm, or nominated to be a knight companion of either of the honourable orders, have fupporters to the arms he has ufed, unlefs he can prove a lawful right to them; and the fame with regard to Efquires, to Knights of the Bath, &c. I mention this to fhew, that however fome from an ill-judged opinion may contemn, or endeavour to difcountenance all things of this kind, there is a time when fuch diftinctions muft be lawfully fettled; and as nothing can excufe a negligence of this fort, every perfon

A a   fhould should be cautious of bearing falſe arms; he ſhould conſider theſe things in due time, that his children may not hereafter be under the neceſſity of ſettling what their father might or ſhould have done before. One would think it natural for every one who had creditably advanced himſelf in fortune to covet ſomething adequate in honour; and it is certain, that he who by his induſtry, his more extenſive and proſperous dealings, or by any other honourable methods, is enabled to be a founder or reſtorer of gentility, and ſhall entail a coat of arms upon his family, has a real claim to honour, and ſtimulates his offspring to exert thoſe laudable principles which have deſerved ſuch diſtinction.

Sundry ſtatutes and ordinances have been made by the commands of former kings of this realm concerning arms, particularly King Henry V. in the fifth year of his reign, on his expedition into France, to ſupport the dignity of theſe diſtinctions, by ſpecial prohibition forbid by public proclamation the uſurping of arms; that no perſon in that expedition ſhould preſume to wear any coat-armour to which he had not a right from his anceſtors, or from ſufficient deputy impowered to grant the ſame, under ſevere penalties, except thoſe who bore arms with him at the battle of Agencourt; thereby rewarding his veteran ſoldiers with a mark of honour, as Francis Sandford, Eſq; Lancaſter Herald, obſerves in his Genealogical Hiſtory, p. 282, where the words of the record may be ſeen.

The

The king also sent his orders to the sheriffs of the several counties not to permit any to bear arms without licence from him, or proper officers deputed to grant the same. In Queen Elizabeth's reign one *Daukins*, for taking upon him the office of a king of arms, was whipped, pilloried, and had his ears cut off. In the 20th of King Charles II. one *Randal Holmes*, a painter, was prosecuted by Norroy king of arms at Stafford assizes for marshalling the funeral, &c. of Sir RALPH ASHTON, and obtained a verdict, with costs and 20 l. damages. Queen Anne, to revive and preserve the ancient honour and esteem due to the nobility and gentry of this kingdom from people of the lower class intruding into their families and usurping their arms, did, for prevention of the same, issue out her command to HENRY Earl of Bindon, then deputy earl marshal of England, to put in execution the statutes and ordinances relating thereto. " In the 13th of King George I. one *Robert Harman*, for assuming the title and office of Herald, was prosecuted by the College of Heralds at the quarter-sessions held at Beccles in Suffolk, and ordered to stand in the pillory in three several towns on public market-days, and afterwards to be imprisoned and fined; which order was accordingly executed." In Scotland, according to an act 12 parliament King Jac. VI. " the moveables and furniture whereon false arms are painted or engraven shall be confiscated, besides the offender to pay 100 l. damages; and in case of failure to be incarcerate." It is not long since the *French* published an order inhibiting the

assumption

assumption of arms not warranted by the laws of that country. Among other resolutions of the lords spiritual and temporal in *Ireland* (Die Lunæ, 6º die Februarii 1758) IT was resolved in parliament, that all persons assuming to themselves titles of honour, or bearing ensigns of honour not warranted by law, nor allowed by the known courtesy of that land, upon their carriages, plate, or furniture, were guilty of a high breach of the privileges of that house, and that it would proceed without delay to punish all such persons who should offend in any of the said premises. IT was ordered also, that the king of arms do from time to time make inquiry after all persons who should afterwards offend in any of the said points, and to make regular returns of the names of all such delinquents to the clerk of the parliament. IT was also ordered by the said lords spiritual and temporal then in parliament assembled, THAT the KING of ARMS, attended by his proper officers, do proceed to blot out and deface all ensigns of honour borne by such persons upon their carriages, plate, furniture, &c. According to the Public Ledger (7th Jan. 1763) " the king of *Sweden* issued an order forbidding all such as are neither Counts, Barons, nor Nobles, to bear the arms of nobility, or open helmets upon their seals, on paying five hundred crowns."

I shall conclude these observations with the following quotation from MAITLAND's History of London (last edit. vol. ii. p. 862, 863); " The OFFICE *of Arms* has subsisted in this
" kingdom

"kingdom five hundred years with reputation: these officers
"had anciently the character of surpassing foreign heralds in
"knowledge and practice. *Hector Boetius* owns that this su-
"periority was universally given them; and *Menstrier*, a French-
"man, acknowledges, that after the *French*, the *English* are
"the most knowing; both writers that cannot be suspected
"of partiality. Nor would it be difficult to enumerate officers
"of arms, of every degree in the College, who have ex-
"celled and distinguished themselves in the respective offices.
"There is not an office of arms in *Europe* where the public
"ceremonial, the arms and pedigrees of families, and all
"other matters relating to the science of HERALDRY, are so
"regularly disposed and so well preserved; and if the descents
"have not been continued so well since the Revolution as be-
"fore, by reason of the discontinuance of visitations and fu-
"neral certificates, it is not the *Heralds* fault; gentlemen
"may supply that defect themselves if they please, the public
"office is always open for that purpose.

"The continuing of descents in the office of arms is not
"only for the honour of families, but of great use and bene-
"fit with regard to their inheritances. Lord Chief Justice *Coke*
"observes, that the dealings of the *Kings of Arms* in descents
"and pedigrees may be a means to quiet many controversies
"about titles of honour, dignities, and inheritances, and this
"is confirmed by experience. The Heralds books have al-

" ways been allowed as evidence at the common law, in the
" house of lords, and in proceedings according to the eccle-
" siastical law; and with regard to precedency, public cere-
" monials, and arms, their books are conclusive.

" As to arms, no person who hath the least knowledge in
" our history or laws can be ignorant of the value put upon
" them by our ancestors, as being the hereditary marks of
" their noblesse: they are the most permanent and lasting ho-
" nours, whereby the memory of families is preserved; many
" of which, but for them, would be buried in oblivion. Lord
" Chief Justice *Coke* speaking of arms asserts, that every gen-
" tleman must be *arma gerens*; and that the best trial of a
" gentleman in blood is by bearing arms; that they are the
" most certain proofs and evidences of nobility and gentry.
" And again, *Nobiles sunt, qui arma gentilitia antecessorum pro-*
" *ferre possunt*. Every gentleman, therefore, must be distin-
" guished by his proper arms, as without arms he cannot be
" a gentleman; nevertheless it is but too common to *apocry-*
" *phate gentlemen* with false or fictitious arms; which, how-
" ever, is not to be wondered at, when we daily observe our
" best laws evaded. Every person who thus usurps arms in-
" vades the prerogative, and very frequently the property of
" another; it is not only dishonourable, but dishonest, and
" an indelible mark of a base mind as well as of a mean ex-
" traction; at the same time, by this instance of low pride,

" he

"he publishes his own dishonour and injures his posterity,
"making them thereby at least one step lower in rank as gen-
"tlemen. But the usurpation of arms is still worse by persons
"in high stations: to see men of the first rank in all profes-
"sions using false or fictitious arms; to see even those who
"ought to enforce the laws of their country acting contrary
"to the laws of arms (which are the laws of the land as
"much as the common law); to see churches, colleges, halls,
"the court, the city, and the camp, displaying false arms, is
"an offence to the Public and a dishonour to the nation.

"There is nothing more universally acknowledged than
"the use of arms; they are the property of gentlemen,
"which ought to be preserved to them inviolable: even those
"who usurp these ensigns of honour, as gentlemen must
"desire, in that respect, to be what they seem; therefore arms
"being duly regulated, and with the pedigrees and descents
"of the bearers recorded in the Heralds Office, must be de-
"sired by every gentleman, would add a lustre even to nobi-
"lity, preserve inheritances, be an honour to the kingdom,
"and a lasting benefit to posterity."

I could here enter into a large discourse concerning the public utility of the Heralds Office; and could easily shew how
prejudicial a disregard to it may prove; but being myself an
Herald, I shall forbear to expatiate on these topics, which

might

might be construed as arising more from a view to private interest than zeal for the public service. Of what use the valuable materials there preserved are and may be, will I hope fully appear from the *Genealogical Tables* of the ENGLISH NOBILITY that will shortly be published in Numbers.

I cannot finish this rude Essay without intreating the indulgence of the candid reader; I am conscious of its many imperfections; but the constant attendance on the duties of my office, and the many avocations to which I am subject, have prevented me from treating the matter in hand with that precision and regularity I could have wished. The subject is indeed of importance; and I shall be extremely happy, if the *loose Hints* here thrown out should induce some more masterly hand to give them that force and order which the nature of them undoubtedly deserve.

FINIS.

HERALDS OFFICE, May 1, 1764.

Shortly will be Published in Numbers,

BARONAGIUM ANGLIÆ;

SIVE

STEMMATA NOBILITATIS ANGLICANÆ:

Exhibiting, in a regular Series of Defcents,

The GENEALOGIES of the ENGLISH NOBILITY,
With Hiftorical Notes occafionally introduced.

EMBELLISHED WITH

Efcutcheons of Arms, Crefts, Supporters, Mottos, Badges, &c.

The Whole confirmed by authentic Monuments of Antiquity preferved in the Public Offices of the Kingdom, particularly in the College of Arms.

By { RALPH BIGLAND, Efq; Somerfet
AND
ISAAC HEARD, Efq; Lancafter } Heralds.

This Work will be rendered ftill more complete by the Addition of the DESCENTS of the feveral HEIRESSES,

(A Plan hitherto unattempted)

WHEREBY

The extenfive Alliances of each NOBLE FAMILY, additional Titles, Hereditary Honours, Affumption of Arms, Claims to, and Inheritance of Eftates, &c. &c. will be further illuftrated.

CONDITIONS.

I. THIS WORK will be printed in Folio upon a large superfine Imperial Paper, and will make about FIFTY Numbers.

II. EACH NUMBER, containing EIGHT Pages, ſtitched in Blue, will be publiſhed as often as the Nature of the Work will admit, Price FOUR SHILLINGS.

III. EACH SUBSCRIBER to pay TWO GUINEAS in Advance on account of the great Expence that will attend the Execution of the Work; this Money will be allowed in the Numbers delivered.

IV. A LIST of the Subſcribers will be Printed.

The NOBILITY and GENTRY who are inclined to patronize this Work, are deſired to ſend their Names and Subſcription-Money as early as poſſible to the COMPILERS at the Heralds Office, by whom the Numbers will be regularly delivered, as well as by the following Bookſellers;

R. and J. DODSLEY, in Pall-mall.
R. DAVIS, in Piccadilly.
J. ROBSON, in New Bond-ſtreet.
J. GRETTON, in Old Bond-ſtreet.
T. PAYNE, at the Mews Gate.
T. DAVIES, in Ruſſell-ſtreet, Covent-Garden.
W. BATHOE, in the Strand.
A. WESLEY, in Holborn.
J. STEPHENS, between the Temple Gates
T. SNELLING, in Fleet-ſtreet.
G. KEARSLEY, in Ludgate-ſtreet.
J. RIVINGTON, } St. Paul's Church-yard.
W. BRISTOW, }
H. PAYNE, in Pater-noſter-Row.
T. FIELD, the upper End of Cheapſide
RICHARDSON and URQUHART, at the Royal Exchange.

Where SPECIMENS of the Work may be ſeen.